THE GOOD SOLDIERS

WILLIAM B. MOODY
CDR CHC USNR-RETIRED

THE GOOD SOLDIERS

"LOOK AWAY
TO DISTANT HILLS
WHILE THEY'RE BATHED IN LIGHT."

GOOD SOLDIERS
PUBLISHING
WACO, TEXAS

Copyright © by Good Soldiers Publications
All rights reserved

Library of Congress Cataloging in Publication Data
Moody, William B., 1925-
The good soldiers.
1. Vietnamese Conflict, 1961-1975, United
States
2. Title. DS558.M66 1986
959.704'3373   86-4656

ISBN.   0-9616499-0-9
Printed in the United States of America

Good Soldier Publications
4817 Crestwood
Waco, Texas 76710

Dedicated
To
Bobbie
My wife of 36 years and the
best Good Soldier I know.

ACKNOWLEDGEMENTS

Mrs. Tommy (Linda) Turner, Jr.

Without her friendship and encouragement this book would never have been written. Editing. Rewrite.

Mrs. Bruce (Jane) Williams.

Editing.

Major General Carl W. Hoffman, USMC • Retired

This man is one of my heroes. In my eyes he is a role model for every American. His agreement to write the foreword for this book is among the truly great honors I could ever receive.

Mr. Shaw's painting "Look Away To Distant Hills" was inspired by the poem by Chaplain Moody. A 23" × 17" limited edition print of the painting is available from Good Soldier Publications, 4817 Crestwood, Waco, Texas 76710.

FOREWORD

"The Good Soldiers" is a story without a beginning or end. It is a story as old as our Nation, a story as new as the young men and women who are joining the military — TODAY — to serve. Above all, "The Good Soldiers" is a love story, describing through a series of vignettes the unabashed love American servicemen and their families feel for the United States of America.

Seen through the eyes and heard through the ears and felt through the senses of a dedicated Navy chaplain, "The Good Soldiers" tells us of the silent sacrifice, the endless devotion, the heart-rending tragedy of combat. Yet the author assures us of the nobility of the cause, a nobility recognized and exalted by the human beings whose deeds he honors.

The reader will quickly discover that the "Good Soldiers" were not supermen; indeed, they had to conquer the terror that hides in all of us. Realizing this, we gain even greater respect and admiration for those who somehow move forward and upward even while their senses are urging them to turn and run.

Chaplin "Bill" Moody has provided a series of literary sketches that describe with sensitivity and — yes — love some of the "Good Soldiers" he encountered in Vietnam combat, in hospitals, on board ships, and in garison environs. He does not dwell on their motivations or what made them "tick." But the message emerges in bold relief: "The Good Soldiers" were driven — are driven — by their love for God and country.

Bill Moody knows whereof he speaks. He trod the same paths of fear and revulsion, the same trails of doubt and uncertainty, the same highways of honor and glory as "The Good Soldiers" he describes. Underpinned by an abiding faith and the firm conviction that, given the opportunity, his Maker would show him the way, he found divine inspiration in the assurance that his endeavors as a chaplain were of value only as God was allowed to work through him.

Let there be no doubt, Bill Moody is himself one of "The Good Soldiers".

Carl W. Hoffman
Major General, USMC (Retired)

PREFACE

In all our wars, the shameful acts of some Americans have embarrassed the rest of us—while the exemplary actions of "quiet heroes" have gone unnoticed. Honor is due and needful to the noble men and women whose actions were heroic. In this book I offer that honor and respect by sharing some of the incidents I witnessed. Most of the stories I share here come out of the Vietnam conflict, since my heart is most heavy with memories of those days. My perspectives have grown from experiences as an enlisted Marine in World War II and later as a chaplain during the postwar era and in Vietnam.

In the following pages are people I recall, some crushed by life's circumstances, never to recover, and still others, caught up in circumstances beyond their control, who have coped admirably. I remember Panama Charlie who had no arms until American servicemen saw to it that he was fitted with artificial limbs. I treasure memories of a Black Irishman's "Happy Hour." I carry the lessons learned from commanding officers who hurt with and grieved for their men. There were those who changed the lives of thousands of Vietnamese children by establishing orphanages and opening schools. There were men who were a good influence and role model for the younger men who fought by their side. And there were the women whose hours of waiting never cease. In the midst of a nightmare of terror . . . in a war misunderstood and with questions still lingering, I met people, who by their deeds and indomitable spirit could only be described as "the good soldiers." Let their stories make my point . . . honor is due.

THE GOOD SOLDIERS

I
Freedom Is Fragile

VIETNAM: 1965

"Come on, Padre, let's go!"

It was not unusual for the battalion commander to drive up to me and give such an order. I had learned to judge by the tone of his voice whether or not he was serious, or if we were about to engage in some time passing exercise.

"What's going on?" I asked.

"I'm not sure," he replied, "but some of our men are hurt bad!"

The commanding officer was a lieutenant colonel; he was tall, lean and crew-cut. Complete with moustache, his appearance was exactly what you might imagine a career Marine officer to look like. Normally very cautious about every move he made, the C.O. was driving his jeep with a reckless abandon that indicated a serious concern. I was hanging on for dear life as military vehicles are not built for comfort and the roads off the main highways were far from smooth. I had learned that where his men were concerned, he always responded without delay. It took about thirty minutes to reach the isolated outpost where the incident had occurred, a trip that usually took an hour to make. The place was a shambles, giving the appearance of a major battleground. Situated on a little knoll, the outpost gave those who occupied it a commanding view of the terrain about two miles off into the distance. Small pine trees were the dominant growth, and the need-

3

les shed by those trees covered the sandy ground.
The only structure of any kind on the knoll was a
sandbag bunker. There was room inside the bunker
for about six men at one time. Little slits just big
enough to poke an M-16 rifle through had been left
between some of the sandbags. Smoke filled the air
all around us as we screeched to a stop on top of the
little hill. I noticed several trees had been shattered.
Over by the bunker, three bodies covered with blan-
kets were stretched out on the sand. Near the shattered trees eight more were laid out side by side. Behind the bunker, another was propped up in a sitting
position with an opened can of "C" rations resting at
his feet. The dozen men who were left were stum-
bling about the camp straightening up. Most of
them were in a state of shock. I jumped out of the
jeep and hurried over to one of the younger men. He
seemed to be in a daze and his eyes were filled with
tears.

I heard the C.O. cursing and when I learned why,
I could not blame him. An observation plane had become disoriented and mistook the outpost for an
enemy position. An air strike was ordered on our
own outpost. Now, twelve men were dead by mis-
take. His anger vented in a flurry of rage, the Colonel now began to cry "Oh, God, Oh, God!" Perhaps
he was already thinking of the letters of condolence
we would have to write the next day. I could tell he
was hurting as much as anyone there. His grief was
not mistaken for weakness; his men recognized it for
what it was, a deep concern for them. I shifted my
attention to the men and moved from one to another. The words I heard coming out of my mouth
sounded like muffled thumps on a drum, meaning-
less and empty. I was frantic. I was supposed to say
something that would help these men come out of

this tragedy and carry on. Words that should have come easy from years of counseling and compassionate ministry were buried in a moment of utter helplessness. I thought how comforting it would be if someone would just come and put an arm around me. It then occurred to me that if that is what I needed, then perhaps that would be what these young men needed, too. So we hugged one another and wept.

In a few moments, the C.O. and I were in the jeep on our way back to our base camp at Chu Lai. For the most part, the return was a quiet trip, much slower and with little conversation. We did, however, set the time for the memorial service to be conducted the next day. It was to be at one o'clock, December 17, 1965. I remember thinking, "What a way to celebrate Christma ." By the time we arrived at Chu Lai it had begun to rain. We were painted red with the wet clay fanned into the open vehicle by the wheels. Darkness was approaching, and since no lights were allowed after dark for security reasons, I began to be concerned about the conditions affecting the preparations I needed to make for the memorial service the next day. That time had to be special. It was completely dark by the time I settled into work. I spread my poncho out over my head and with the rain pouring down began to scratch through my gear searching for a dry piece of paper. The humidity had curled every piece of dry paper and rendered nearly every pen useless. I did find a dry paper sack which had once contained several cartons of Kool Aid sent to our battalion by a little girl from Oakland, California. While searching for the best place on the sack to begin writing my notes, my flashlight seemed to freeze on words scribbled faintly in pencil . . . "Freedom is fragile, Handle with prayer!" The words had

5

obviously been written by a child. That was it! That statement would be my theme. A poem came easily with those words. After covering virtually every square inch of that sack with notes, I concluded with the poem.

By twelve-forty-five the next day, all the men who were free to come had gathered for the service. An area under some pine trees had been set aside for worship services. There was only room for about twenty men to sit in the shade of the fly-tent stretched out between the trees. This day there must have been two hundred men. They stacked their weapons nearby and sat quietly. My talk was lengthy, but I felt that attention was good. A bond that would grow between these men and me was fashioned that day. We were dismissed following a concluding hymn and prayer, and the men returned to their respective duties. We were scattered over a large area and some of the men had only limited time to get back to their tasks. One of the Marines asked for a copy of the poem I had read. I was so grateful that something had been said which he wanted to remember that I handed him the sack, notes and all. That was the last I saw of it until to my surprise, about three months later, *The Oakland Tribune, The Philadelphia Inquirer,* and *The Arlington (Texas) Citizen* all published the entire presentation. It is reproduced here with the hope that it will be as meaningful now as some thought it was then, and to provide a setting for everything that follows on these pages. As you read it, remember the occasion for the memorial service. Twelve men had been slain. American involvement in Vietnam was intensifying. Much confusion existed in the minds of some of our men as they were torn between their duty here and the protests they knew were occurring on the streets of America. Ugliness and hatred dominated many of those demonstrations. The vilification of any who disagreed with those protestors is well documented. These factors made the strain on the men in South Vietnam and on their families at home much greater than it would otherwise have been. The dichotomy of protest and duty, added to the immediate loss felt by the battalion, may give some clue as to the feelings which prevailed at that moment. Go back with me now to South Vietnam, December 17, 1965, and share one hour with us at the memorial service . . .

Memorial Service
Twelve Marines
December 17, 1965

Pick up a newspaper in your hometown or city. Somewhere on the front page you will find a strong protest or firm approval of our involvement in South Vietnam. Far too few reports of either view include any real idea of what this land, its people, or the Americans here are all about. Some are content to remain ignorant and pretend that this whole ugly mess just does not exist. From our uncomfortable vantage point, we can observe that many of the voices for or against our involvement take their position in whatever choir sings in the key best suited to their particular philosophical tune. This is easy to do when they have a city in which to live, have a family, worship or not worship, demonstrate or petition their government, or generally do as they please. The privileges just mentioned are not enjoyed by the people all around us where even their basic needs often go unmet. Here, you men see a different picture each day. The South Vietnamese peo-

7

ple are much like those described in Psalm 107:4, a people who "wandered in a wilderness in a solitary way; they found no city to dwell in. Hungry and thirsty their soul fainted within them." Any Vietnamese who has even the faintest semblance of a permanent residence, has learned through long years of war, that nothing is theirs for very long. I remind you, in contrast, that in the United States, even the poorest have much to be thankful for. Even those Americans caught up in circumstances that leave them destitute and without much hope to control their situation, have access to assistance and support.

Among the affluent, there are some examples of persons who have forgotten the cost with which their ease was purchased. Some may be too young to remember, but others seem to be just too dull to appreciate the fact that our heritage has been bought with the lives of young men, all of whom hated every minute of the wars they fought.

Today's conflict in this place is a part of history where the need to defend freedom is being challenged. However, I predict that this challenging will manifest itself in a record of nobility and courage. All of you with whom I am privileged to serve speak to one another about going back to the "real world" (United States). It is the land of the "Big P.X." where you have a home and a city in which to dwell. Any of you, if I were to ask, could tell me how many more days you have here before you head for home.

None of us is qualified to engage in political arguments as to why we should be here at all. But I have, and you certainly have, unique qualifications to speak from a special viewpoint. Years from now people still will not understand, and you will know some things impossible for them to know. Veterans of this conflict will meet one an other on the streets of the "real world" in expressions of affection understood only by those who have been here.

History has taught us that Christian principles are woven into the very fabric of America. Those persons who preside over our government and who base their judgments and decisions on this foundation and its principles, will prove to be our nation's truly great leaders. I would never rationalize our government's position or seek to justify its actions, but the premise that we are a caring nation is the basis on which we honor our friends here today.

Jesus related the story of a man who was set upon by thieves as he journeyed to the city of Jericho. In that familiar story can be seen three basic philosophies of life. The first is epitomized by the thieves, who by their actions were saying, "What is yours is mine, and I am going to take it from you." Then there came on the scene certain individuals who, to say the least, had religious connections. They passed by on the other side of the road, in effect saying "What is mine is mine, and I am going to keep it." Finally, the third philosophy is represented by the man who stopped to help the one who had been a victim of thieves. His attitude was, "What's mine is yours, and I am going to share it with you."

I have no problem whatsoever in drawing a comparison with where we are today and that third philosophy of life. The history of America is written in deeds of sharing and caring for the less fortunate.

I see people around us half dead and ruled by tyranny. Some outsiders have tried to walk by on the other side of the road, while others simply choose to ignore the victim and avoid involvement. I see people who have not had much hope for a long time. Now, they are breaking out their flag and flying it for the first time in years. Schools that have been closed are being reopened because of your presence. Like the Samaritan, you have shared yourselves and you are making a difference.

The great majority of these people are not properly represented to the world by the advertisements purported to portray the Vietnamese. The romantic little brochure showing an attractive young woman in native costume riding a bicycle through the countryside does not show the typical female of this nation. Nor is a little sailboat, propelled by a summer breeze down the river at Hue, a picture of the way the average citizen here might spend his time.

Nearer the truth are the haggard women, idle men and undernourished children with fear on their faces. They represent the masses of peasants and farmers who constitute the majority population of this land, and who are pawns in a civil war about which they know very little. Some critics might say that what we are attempting to do is a hopeless effort, but we must remind ourselves that though success is not always guaranteed in such efforts, the trying is what we must value, particularly if we are to maintain the freedoms now a part of our way of life.

Near here is a village you have named "No Name Village". It is a place without a name, and cannot be found on a map. Nobody cares. It is indicative of a forgotten cluster of people viewed by themselves and others as being so insignificant that not even a name is given to the place they call home. Speaking of "no city to dwell in," how typical of the people we see here every day. Contrast the child of six years here and his counterpart in your hometown. Instead of playing children's games or going to nursery school, the child here carries a baby sister or brother on his hip most of the day or a burden two to three times his own weight on his back.

Shoes, soap, and other incidentals are sought after treasures, and you are supplying many of those things to them. Babies with open sores are literally attacked by swarms of flies. Indoor toilets in open boxes are often seen inches away from a babe eating rice from a bowl. You have entered their lives, teaching the basic rules of hygiene. People who never come here will not believe these stories, but your appreciation of the towns and cities we dwell in, will be enhanced by having been here.

Families have been impaled on stakes because they expressed a determination to be free to make their own choices. Their courage has encouraged you to establish, or at least assist in the process of setting up, refugee villages. Those kinds of deeds are no less than giving some of these people, if only for a brief moment in their lives, "a city to dwell in."

We are on that side of the Jericho road that costs something. On this particular day, we do not need to be reminded of what that cost is, but we will always remember that it was laid out on the sands of Chu Lai, Pleiku, and Danang. None of these men wanted to die. They wanted to go back to their homes, their cities and dwell there in peace.

I've watched you help people by day and then spend your nights in a rice paddy or the underbrush. Hoping for rest, you most usually received a visit from a mongoose, rat or bamboo snake . . . all rousing your tired bodies with new desires to go home. The price is high, but it always has been. History has taught us and underscored those lessons with sacrifice, that those who will not fight aggression wherever they find it will not long remain free themselves. Only as we lend our strength to help others have their own cities to dwell in without fear, can the world ever expect to rest from its struggles.

Sadly, more men will have to die. Letters of condolence will interrupt the dreams of families at home, and men like you will attend memorial services like this one. Accompanying those letters will be broken homes, and for some, unforgettable nightmares of a new-found friend suddenly gone. There will be many who will not know of, or will not hear or remember those sacrifices. But the important thing is that WE do not forget. The memory of these fallen men will survive the indifference of those who are everlastingly content to pass by "on the other side of the road."

We will not forget, because the wounds of our comrades are our wounds, too.

Think for a moment on the emptiness of the words, "no city to dwell in." What price is right to see that that can never be said of you and yours? We cannot, we must not forget, for the sake of these we remember here today, that "Freedom is Fragile!"

FREEDOM IS FRAGILE

Christmas comes but once a year
With its Christ-child and His good cheer.

But from this land by war so torn
Where fear and death stalk each newborn;

Where women die young from toils so great
And promise their children an unknown fate;

We remember the blessings of our great land
And dare to fight and take a stand.

So with our loved ones this thought we share;
"Freedom is fragile, Handle with Prayer."

II
A View From The Heart

The Armor of God
EPHESIANS 6:14-17

A VIEW FROM THE HEART
VIETNAM: 1965

The plane was circling for a landing. From my seat by the window "I" could see could see Okinawa below. We had been told we would land there for a briefing and shots before going on to South Vietnam. As the aircraft settled into a landing pattern, I could make out the lush green growth of the area. I searched for a familiar landmark. I saw nothing recognizable, however, since my only other visit to the island had taken place almost twenty years before when I had been an enlisted Marine among those who had made the initial landings on this island to wrest it from Japanese control.

Thoughts of that action raced through my brain. I was nineteen years younger then, and I remembered almost jealously that I had also been a "whole bunch of pounds" lighter. I had weighed only about 120 pounds. An audible chuckle emerged as I also remembered that in those days I carried a twenty-one pound weapon, a Browning Automatic Rifle (BAR), along with the seventy-two pounds of ammunition that went with it. All these thoughts were of a much younger man, almost as if I was thinking of someone other than myself. Being a Marine in World War II was a source of real pride for me. That war, unlike the conflict in Vietnam, was one in which nearly every American had played an active role.

The short stay on Okinawa ended and the

17

thoughts generated upon arrival were gone very quickly. Soon, the plane was circling for another landing. This time it was Danang, South Vietnam. Nothing, of course, was familiar, although I was surprised to see a large number of South Vietnamese regulars armed with BARs. Some things had not changed. Chaplains are noncombatants and not allowed to bear arms, so the weapons made little difference to me this time. As I stepped from the plane I experienced a vast difference in my feelings about being in a war zone at this point in my life from those feelings remembered from World War II. My priorities had undergone a giant shift toward caution. "Home" for me now included wife and children. Something else was new, too. I was angry over the shouts of demonstrators and the confusion they heaped on these young men so far away from home and so near to the terrors of war.

After a brief period of time used to settle in, I was introduced to Chaplain Gordon Cook, the man I was replacing. This man had been a genuine inspiration to the men of the battalion. As I quickly learned the ropes of my new assignment and met the men, I began to understand why he was so respected. He had shared himself with his men and maintained a demanding schedule which kept him closely in touch with their needs.

Everyone had some initial problems getting accustomed to the food and climate, but after I had made these normal adjustments, the inevitable rawness of war became a reality. "Bedcheck Charlie" was a nickname given to a sniper who regularly visited around midnight. Some lone sniper would fire small arms into the camp just to harass us and keep everyone on his toes. Snipers employed lots of tricks to prevent the flash from their weapons from being seen . . . such as firing from behind an umbrella.

The day soon came when I accompanied two of our companies on a major sweep through enemy territory. We were transported by amphibious vehicles part of the way, then moved on foot to the target area. We heard land mines and booby traps exploding in the distance, and we received reports of several casualties. Things quieted considerably as we moved ahead toward a rendezvous area. Suddenly, sounding like electrical wires carrying a heavy load, small arms fire burst from all directions. At that moment I realized what a good target the cross on my helmet made of me. Another thought surfaced, too. If we were overrun, I had no way to defend myself.

The operation ended almost as soon as it had begun, with no one knowing too much about what was accomplished. I was inundated with thoughts about how much more comfortable I would be with a "security blanket," a .45 caliber side arm. I had felt bound by the regulations concerning chaplains bearing arms. Perhaps now it was time to quit playing games and acting brave and to prepare for the next such encounter. With these thoughts racing through my mind, I marched briskly towards the supply tent to check out a weapon. I signed all the papers, strapped on the .45 and headed toward the tent entrance. Through the flaps I could see four black Marines engaged in animated conversation. To get to my place would take me right across their path, and I knew that they knew I was not supposed to have a weapon. I could not go out of that tent with that pistol.

I marched back to the counter, returned the weapon, and was never again tempted to bear arms. I recall that experience because of what immediately followed. Making my way out into the sunshine, I glanced toward my tent, just beyond the point where the Marines were standing. Just five feet from where I slept at night, men were positioning a heavy mortar. Little did I know that before the night was over, I would discover that when that weapon fired, the earth nearby acted like a trampoline. I also learned that I could jump real high from a prone position if that weapon fired when I was not expecting it.

My attention probably would have remained riveted on the mortar team's activity had not the loud talking of the four Marines distracted me. As I drew nearer I could catch bits and pieces of their very intense conversation. The three men doing all the listening noticed my approach and tried unsuccessfully to get the one doing all the talking to be quiet. (I was always amused at how quickly a conversation could take a different turn with the appearance of a chaplain.) The speaker, with his back to me, got louder with every word. Even though I overheard the names "God" and "Jesus Christ" mentioned several times, I knew their conversation was not about religion. By this time I was only an arm's length away. Even as he continued speaking, I placed my hand on his shoulder and said, "My man, you will never know how inspiring it is for a chaplain to drop in on his men and hear them talking about God. In fact, I am so moved, may I invite you to kneel right here with me while we ask Him to bless our ministry together?" We did that and, as it later turned out, He did bless our ministry together. We became great friends and shared much more in the days to come.

Waiting is always a part of military life. On a particular day a large part of our battalion were in full battle gear and assembled at the airfield. The

"Jolly Green Giant" helicopters that were to move us to a place we called "Happy Valley" were late, and several hundred men were lying around on their packs just waiting it out. The name of our destination, "Happy Valley," was deceiving. Reports from other exercises in that area had always included long lists of casualties. So, this particular waiting time had special unspoken significance and undoubtedly produced some special thoughts in the minds of every man there.

I glanced around to see how the men were passing their time. Some were asleep, or appeared to be. Others were examining the sand at their feet. (Sand was always a curious subject of conversation. The sand at Chu Lai had grains that were round instead of angular, which made it almost impossible to put a tent pole in the ground. It was like trying to make the pole stand up in water.) Some were writing letters although there would be no opportunity to mail them. About that time I spotted my four Marines. They were by themselves and as usual appeared quite busy.

As I walked toward them I noticed they were playing with some dice. Now that was against the rules, but the military currency they were playing with wasn't going anywhere anyway; besides, their minds were better spent on that than in thinking of what might lie ahead for them. However, I couldn't resist giving them a hard time. I had allowed them to make me the friendly target of some of their pranks, and now it was my turn. When I got close enough, I leaned over, scooped up their money and the dice and said, "Thanks, guys, for your contribution to the chapel fund." They laughed, but became very serious as I began chiding them about the evils of gambling. Keeping up the ruse, I then called their attention to the fact that they did not really have any skill with the dice. I would give them a lesson.

"Watch this!" I said, as I threw the dice out on the blanket at their feet. The dice rolled to an easy "seven." They couldn't believe it, and I didn't let on that I was nearly as surprised as they were. They dared me to try it again. Nonchalantly, and thinking the charade was over, I picked up the dice once more and, tossing them between my legs, said, "Watch this trick shot!" Would you believe another "seven"? They were amazed ... and so was I. Naturally, they encouraged me to do it just once more, but I could see the handwriting on the wall, and refused to destroy their faith in me bygoing for it a third time. From that moment on, for a long period of time, they looked upon me as a kind of "good luck charm." During the weeks and months that passed, they all grew in a genuine faith. Before we went our separate ways, I had the privilege of baptizing all four of them in the South China Sea.

I felt I had been able to do something for those men. In return, those four Marines, for as long as we were together, unless they were otherwise assigned, positioned themselves near me when dangerous situations arose. They were giving so much of themselves, far more than they knew, without knowing why they were here in this country halfway across the world.

WHERE ARE YOU, JIM?

I wish there was some way I could locate him, this special guy named Jim. He was always around when needed. He had been appointed Protestant Lay Leader for his company and always arranged a place for our meeting when I came. Jim, a sergeant, was older than most of the noncommissioned officers of equal rank. He had been blessed with a deep bass voice and, although he had had no formal training, he could sing old hymns with a depth of feeling that inspired everyone. Our services always began with Jim singing "Amazing Grace." Any chaplain would have been delighted to have this man around. My wife has always said that my singing was like "asthma set to music." Evidently the men in Charley Company thought so too and were glad Jim was there. He loved everybody, and many times I overheard him sharing some very wise thoughts with the younger men. Jim, a black man, was one of the tenderest, most caring people I have ever known. He reminded me of many things I had learned as a child and was just now beginning to understand deeply and maturely.

After a particularly moving experience of hearing Jim sing at one of our services, his company was scheduled to move out in a brief operation where casualties were expected to be heavy. I watched them leave, and the last man I saw was Jim with a big toothy grin on his face and a thumbs up signal to me. After they were gone, everyone who could kept checking with our communications people to keep up with reported casualties or whatever other news came in. Late that evening word came that two choppers would be bringing in wounded. When the two "birds" finally arrived, I recognized the big hulk of Jim being lifted from the second chopper. He was rushed into the aid station where corpsmen began preparing him for treatment. I tried to stand close enough to see and still be out of the way. When they pulled the wet fatigues from his body, I saw that his abdomen was laid open and his insides were visible. He had lain in a rice paddy for some time after being wounded and was chilled to the bone. He was still conscious and the pain and chill combined to make it impossible for him to relax. Shots he needed were nearly impossible to administer because every nerve and muscle was taut. He glanced in my direction and I caught a look on his face that I would never have expected to see there. He was afraid.

I had learned how important it was to avoid distracting medical teams when they were working. Never did I see anything but the tenderest and most caring attention given to our wounded. In this instance I sensed a helplessness in their futile efforts to get Jim to relax. One of them turned to me and said, "Pray for him, Padre!" I lifted the New Testament from Jim's torn and bloody jacket and stepped up to the table where they were working. I knew that Jim's faith was far deeper and more obvious than my own. It was apparent that at this moment words of that faith were not as important as was the exercise of that faith. Slipping an arm under his shoulders and holding the Testament where he could see it, I said, "Jim, you have always believed in this book and carried it with you. You have preached more than I have to the young men around you; now it's time for you to practice what you have preached. Let that faith work for you so your wounds can be treated."

We said a short prayer together. Almost immediately he relaxed and, with not such a pretty voice but a sincere one, he began to sing, "Amazing Grace, how sweet the sound." Before he could begin the second phrase he was asleep from the anesthetic. Jim recovered and went home. But he had shown me the power of the faith we shared.

JUST DO WHAT YOU CAN

The weather in Vietnam was a factor in almost everything we did. One part of that little country would be hot and humid, while another would be cool and wet. The monsoons would take their toll in one area while another place could expect them at another time. It wasn't terribly cold but the dampness, coupled with sixty degree temperatures for weeks at a time, made it seem much colder. Many times I thought about how dissatisfied we would become at the weather back in Texas where the old saying "In Texas, if you don't like the weather, just wait a minute and it will change" is certainly true. I decided in 1966 that if I ever got home, I would never complain about the weather again. Chaplain Gordon Cook, whom I had relieved, had set a blistering pace for me to follow despite the weather. His attention and concern for the men of this battalion was unprecedented. With the weather the way it was, it was hard for me to understand how he could have accomplished all he did. He served as an inspiration to me. I tried to find ways to cover the sixty-five square mile territory our units occupied. There were only two jeeps and the one assigned to the commanding officer was not often available to me.

Helicopters that brought water, supplies and mail on regularly scheduled trips from one part of the battalion to another became one of my most frequent modes of travel. Most of the time, however, I moved around on foot, sometimes accompanied by one armed man assigned to me, at other times alone, or met at some halfway point by a squad or more of men from the unit expecting a worship service. On some occasions, the service might be conducted at a bridge and attended by the six to twelve men assigned to protect it. At other times it might be attended by several dozen or even one hundred men or more. For those who attended services, that day, whatever it was, became Sunday. At one time, having worked out a fairly reliable schedule, we were having a worship service every one and one-half hours of daylight time, seven days a week. In that time frame, all, or nearly all, of the men of First and Second Battalions of the Fourth Marine Regiment would have had an opportunity to attend a service. I tried to provide a few minutes at each service to give any of the men an opportunity to talk if they wanted to. The men always showed an eagerness to talk and visit. One occasion that stands out in my mind is of a young Marine NCO who indicated he was extremely anxious to talk. I had noticed his preoccupation with his own thoughts during the worship service.

He was stationed on a little island just fifty meters from the mainland. It was a strange little body of land covered by trees. On one half were palm trees and on the other half were pine trees. A picture of the island from the Chu Lai Peninsula made it look as though someone had planned it that way. The beginning of the pines marked the area used by the Marines as their base. A few yards from their tents and living area was a little place they called their chapel. The ground was thick with pine needles and just feet away was the ocean. On balmy days, this little place was inspiring as the ocean breeze made barely audible sounds in the pines. As we sat on the thick carpet of pine needles, feeling that breeze, and hearing the gentleness of the sounds, we found this an ideal place to worship. There were no pews, stained glass or other trappings, only a sense of His presence.

At the conclusion of the service, I sought out the young man I had noticed during the hymns and sermon. At his request, we found an even more secluded place to visit for a moment. He began by saying that he knew there was probably nothing that could be done about the request he was about to make, but that he just wanted to talk about it.

His concern was one I had heard many times before and even experienced myself. On the previous day he had gotten a letter from his wife telling of the birth of their first child, a little boy. That night, in a very vivid dream, he had seen himself being killed within the week. He wanted to know if there was any chance at all of his being transferred back to the states earlier than scheduled. I wanted to do something for him so badly, but obviously there was nothing that could be done except to say "I know how you feel."

The next day I learned that he was killed in action only hours after our visit. I remembered the prayer we had shared. He had walked with me back to the helicopter as I was leaving. I had not helped him very much and that disturbed me. But I had learned that sometimes we can help and sometimes we can't. Sometimes, we can help best by just being available. We just do what we can.

III
Miracles of Xuan Trang

MIRACLES OF XUAN TRANG

A miracle is a miracle anywhere it occurs. Often the miracle is as much in how it comes to pass as it is the act itself.

Xuan Trang was a typical country village in South Vietnam. The only structures in this community were those with thatched roofs, clay walls and dirt floors. They served as homes by night and shops (if you stretched your imagination) by day. These buildings lined either side of a forty-yard path which served as the town's only street. Traffic consisted of an occasional bicycle or buffalo drawn cart. Scattered around this "business district" were small farms tended by people who called Xuan Trang home. Most of the villagers were related. Traveling through the town was often hampered by the scores of children playing in the road, most of them between the ages of four and eight years. Most seemed to be carrying a younger brother or sister balanced on their hip or back. Older children usually carried heavy burdens such as water for cooking or bathing. Women of all ages usually ran the little shops since there were very few men in the area. Water buffalo served as power for plowing the fields and working the rice paddies. A faint stench filled the air along with smoke from cook fires and burning debris. Xuan Trang was no different from hundreds of other peasant villages dotting the South Vietnamese countryside.

In all of these villages immense need was apparent. Outstretched, dirty little hands begging for anything eloquently spoke of the longing desires for something different from what they had. Little children running along behind jeeps or tugging at the fatigues of American soldiers wrapped themselves around the hearts of many of our military personnel. In any of these country villages, tragedy, despair and primitive lifestyles were common.

PANAMA CHARLIE

From Xuan Trang, a little man with no arms became the subject of a miracle. He was twenty-seven
years old and different, never wearing the traditional "black pajamas" of most other Vietnamese
men. Whenever I saw him he was always wearing
flip-flops, trousers, a blue long sleeved shirt, sunshades and a panama hat. The hat earned him the
nickname of "Panama Charlie." The sunshades hid
from those who did not know - the hole where one of
his eyes had been gouged out by the Viet Cong. The
long sleeved shirt hid nothing as the sleeves flapped
their emptiness in the wind. His arms had been am-
putated, both lost when he was much younger when
a booby trap exploded near him. Charlie was a
prominent member of the village, always visible. But
he was living in a time and place where even mini-
mal medical attention was far away, and where his
great needs could not begin to be met. For anything
good to happen to Panama Charlie a miracle would
have to take place.

Like those of so many of his countrymen, Panama
Charlie's plight was accepted as a fact of life, just
one more in a whole sea of tragedies. Always out-
wardly happy, Charlie seemed to have taken his pre-
dicament in stride. Like many other villagers, he had
learned to appreciate the giving and caring nature of
the Americans he met. Understandably, when it was
rumored that we were leaving the area around Xuan
Trang, this little man grew alarmed. When he first
heard the rumor, Charlie greeted me on my next
visit by wrapping the stubs of his arms around my
waist, crying out, with big tears flowing from under
his sunshades. In words I could not understand, he

spoke with desperation. A local school teacher ran over to interpret. "He is saying he wants to be a whole person." Before you leave can you get him some arms?"

The rumors of our leaving proved false, but the men who had witnessed that scene could not forget Charlie's desperation. They determined that he would be fitted with artificial limbs. Their undying persistence raised enough money to finance a trip to Saigon. There an American doctor fitted Charlie with arms. Because someone cared, a miracle happened to one little man.

OPERATION CLEFT PALATE

But these scenes were not isolated incidents; a little eight-year-old girl, like Panama Charlie, was lost in the sheer numbers of those who needed special, but unavailable, attention. Different from Charlie, her needs were not of man's doing. She suffered from a severe cleft palate, a not unusual affliction among the people of Vietnam. Hers was so acute, however, that most of the time she would hold her arm over her face to escape the unwanted stares. Strangers passing through the village sent her scurrying for a hiding place. It was quite by accident that a Marine caught her by surprise one day face-to-face. That evening when I returned from my rounds, the young Marine was waiting for me. He began telling me with genuine compassion what he had witnessed. Particularly moving to him was the embarrassment he saw on that little disfigured face when she realized she had been seen. Little did she know that that was the best thing that could have happened to her. From his initial compassion grew a ground swell of sacrifice and good will that financed another trip to Saigon. It was one of many such journeys, perhaps hundreds, of children and adults who needed such surgery. So many, in fact, that a project called "Operation Cleft Palate" was organized and financed in part by our fighting forces.

The first journey, though, with the little girl and her mother included Harry, the young Marine who had seen her and made the trip possible, and a hospital corpsman who had been granted permission to make the trip to try to cut through red tape and expedite the surgery. The two men returned in about a week having completed their mission. Two weeks later, Harry was listed among those killed in an engagement with the Viet Cong. About three months later, we learned that the little girl and her mother would be returning to Danang and then home to Xuan Trang. I traveled to Xuan Trang the next day and when I arrived I saw a crowd gathered around the little girl. When she spotted me she instinctively raised her arm to hide her face. Then, with a grin, she lowered her arm and a natural beauty in unnatural circumstances began to blossom. In a short time, she became known to the villagers as the "miracle of Xuan Trang." A very young Marine, thousands of miles from his home, in a little insignificant village in South Vietnam, in a country torn by a vicious war, had made a miraculous difference in her life. These true stories are not only about the Vietnamese, but are also about Marines, physicians, Army and Navy personnel, civilian doctors and nurses who treated the bodies and spirits of forgotten individuals with impartial tenderness. These incidents are miracles of the highest order.

It is ironic that young men of America seen often as bearers of miracles by the Vietnamese were often lumped together with that minority of ugly Americans labeled by our press and pacifists as "baby killers." How the mention of My Lai saddens me! But my pride in the "good soldiers" has never wavered because of the hundreds of Xuan Trangs whose stories never made the newspapers or newscasts.

The child of Xuan Trang was the object of a true miracle. Those who changed her life - doctors, a corpsman, and a young Marine named Harry, who did not live to see how good a soldier he really was - prove that, even in the midst of war, good people make good things happen.

IV
The Happy Hour

THE HAPPY HOUR

He was a Black Irishman. I had heard of him long before I met him. I had never seen a Black Irishman before, and when I did finally meet him, I saw where the term came from. First, he was definitely an Irishman; he never let you forget that. His complexion was darker than the average person's. Bronzed with an eternal tan, he always appeared to have just stepped off the beach. A crew-cut hair style fit him to a tee. This man was tall and wiry with coal-black eyes that penetrated anyone who looked him in the face.

When we first met, the company he commanded was serving as a buffer for the First Battalion, Fourth Marine Regiment. They were positioned on a small island that had easy access from the mainland peninsula of Chu Lai. At low tide, one could almost walk across from the mainland to the beaches of the island. Most of the time a little metal boat called a Jon-boat carried us across. When we would reach the other side, a squad of fifteen or more men would meet us for the three-mile hike to the company camp area. I made that trip about once a week, usually with a bodyguard, to conduct worship services for the men. The Black Irishman seldom attended. He was a faithful Catholic and was always present when the Catholic chaplain visited, but my only contact with him was never more than the courtesy calls I made on him. I had heard that he had a Happy

Hour every day, and since I was a teetotaler and assumed that his Happy Hour included beer, I thought I understood why he never invited me for a visit. Curiously, in combat zones you can't always get toothpaste, soap or bullets, but beer is always available.

All those preconceived notions about what went on at his Happy Hour changed one day. The helicopter that brought in water and other supplies on a regular schedule was also to serve as my transportation home on this day. I missed it, and when the Black Irishman learned of my dilemma, he cordially invited me in for a Happy Hour while arrangements were being made for me to get back to the home base. Was I ever in for a surprise! There was no beer. This Happy Hour was contained in a small box. It consisted of anchovies, sardines, an assortment of dips and cheeses; real treats that came almost every week packed with care by his wife and five children, one of whom he had never seen.

I realized what I had been missing. We became fast friends after that and I enjoyed many Happy Hours with him. I came to know his children by name, watched him cast loving glances towards his wife's picture, and over a short period of time learned that he was a loving caring man.

I have thought many times since how we often fail to learn about people because we perceive them as being too different from ourselves. Particularly in the situation we were in, I learned that he and I had the same fears, concerns, and hopes. We shared with all the other men the thoughts of being with loved ones again, counting the days until we could each assume whatever was normal to us once again. I also saw that he had a genuine concern for every man in his company.

At some point late in his thirteen-month tour, his responsibilities shifted from the little island to the peninsula coastline, a part of which was very rugged with jagged rocks and sometimes treacherous breakers. This was in stark contrast to the virgin beaches and calm waters between the island and the mainland. Even after this move, I had a standing invitation to his Happy Hour. In just a short time after that change of duties, his relief reported and the time was at hand for the major to return home. On the day before he was to leave South Vietnam for home and his family, the Black Irishman, his relief and I had one last Happy Hour together. Afterwards, I returned to our home base, and the Black Irishman took his relief over the rugged coastline to familiarize the new man with his territory. Just as I arrived at Chu Lai, that old familiar scene occurred again. The battalion commander's jeep slid to a stop nearby and the Colonel shouted, "Saddle up, Chaplain, let's go!" As I climbed into the jeep I asked, "Where are we going?" "I really don't know for sure," he replied. "All I know is that something has happened on the beach, someone slipped on the rocks." My heart jumped. In a moment we were on the beach. Boats were moving up and down the coastline while divers were searching everywhere for a body. I could see the Black Irishman's relief standing on the rocks, alone, looking out to the sea in stunned disbelief. Strong breakers had struck the men as they walked the coastline among the rocks and the Black Irishman had lost his footing. His body was never recovered.

God rest you, my friend, and give you peace.

Chaps

43

V
The Desert Wedding

THE DESERT WEDDING

I have a souvenir of the Kentucky Derby, a sterling silver mint julep cup with a horse's head formed on the side. I use that cup often, not to drink from, but as a starting point for some choice reminiscing. During the summer months of 1969 I was stationed at the Marine Corps Base, Twenty-nine Palms, California. My first tour in the Navy as a chaplain had been at this same base in 1960. My wife and I really loved it, and we were fortunate to meet some really great people on both tours of duty.

Each summer the reserves come to Twenty-nine Palms for their two-weeks active duty. This base is used for artillery training and the expanse of desert land is ideal for maneuvers. To provide realism in their training, the troops are divided into opposing forces. The base furnishes personnel to assist in those exercises and occasionally a chaplain becomes involved. This particular year, I was assigned to work with one of the units. Also involved were some Marines who were American Indians used in ways which utilized their native skills. Their assignment during those maneuvers was to harrass both sides. To be captured by these men was the height of embarrassment. As fate would have it, I was in a jeep with a driver and a hospital corpsman returning from the aid station one day, when out from behind some rocks jumped the Indians. For all practical purposes we were "captured." The first thing done

47

in such a situation is the identification and tagging of the prisoners. We were still sitting in the jeep, motor running, when I realized that our captors were almost in hysterics because they had captured a chaplain.

On a hunch I asked, "Are you men Catholic?"

"Yes, Father," they dutifully replied.

I whispered to the driver to keep the motor running, and turned to the Indians again, asking, "How long has it been since you have been to Mass?" Their reply was welcomed since they admitted it had been a long time. Trying really hard to keep a straight face, and wanting desperately to avoid the ribbing I knew we would get later, I began to give instructions.

"You men line up over here. Kneel down in a row and begin saying your prayers. I'll get set up with a very special service for you."

They did as I told them, and that's the last we saw of them as we sped away in a cloud of dust.

Years later when my family and I returned to Twenty-nine Palms, one of the first things we learned as we took a look at the base newspaper was that the reserves were due back for maneuvers. One of the lead stories "Will the Phantom Chaplain Strike Again?" was a big surprise. Since ten years had passed, I felt free to confess.

Among the reserves who came to the base that year was a young Marine lieutenant from Kentucky and his fiance'. They planned to marry during his two-week training period. They were both school teachers. He was very handsome and she was a special young woman of unusual beauty. They met with the Presbyterian minister from Twenty-nine Palms for counseling sessions and to make plans for the wedding. The townspeople looked upon the wedding as a big event, and most of the parishioners of the church really got involved. All the attention was really more than the couple had bargained for and they began to experience "cold feet." The day before the wedding, they canceled the ceremony in town and asked me to marry them in my office. I agreed, but when that pretty little girl brought her lace wedding gown in for me to see, I could not imagine a ceremony taking place in my very drab office. This was at ten o'clock in the morning, and we had set the time for the ceremony at two o'clock that afternoon.

At one o'clock I began to work some changes to enhance the ceremony a little without violating the couple's wishes to reduce the hubbub. I really kept faith with them until one-thirty when I picked up the phone and called the commanding general, Major General Carl W. Hoffman. When he answered, I asked, "General, how would you like to give a bride away at a wedding?" I briefed him on the situation and when he asked about the time this was to take place, I answered, "In fifteen minutes, sir!" Without hesitation he said, "I'll be there!"

He arrived right on time bringing with him a secretary who was to be maid of honor, the base photographer and a sack of rice he had picked up from the mess hall on his way to the chapel. Also in tow was his chief of staff who was to be the best man. In the time between my call to the general's office and the bride's arrival, we had conscripted a musician who came from the swimming pool in a wet bathing suit and terrycloth robe and proved to be a fine organist. An officer who we knew could sing was spotted in a tank headed out to the training area. We grabbed him up to be the vocalist. It was absolutely one of the sweetest weddings I can remember. But to me, the one thing that made it so special was

General Hoffman.

I had learned a long time ago that most flag rank officers possessed very special characteristics. The availability and kindness of General Hoffman epitomizes many of those special men. He played a trumpet that rivaled Herb Alpert and loved to entertain. He represented to me the ultimate in a military officer. Some officers thought that yelling and screaming orders sprinkled with a due amount of profanity was part of the image they need to project. Not this man. His authority was on his shoulders with his designation of rank. That was all he needed, because he was obviously a man of great intelligence, dignity and genuine concern for the men in his command. His willingness to participate in the wedding of people he barely knew demonstrated the extraordinary qualities of this leader.

A commanding officer in combat is sometimes perceived as callous and disinterested in what happens to his men. This is not only a false perception, but I believe it to be contrary to the norm. These men grieve with every casualty and ache with each painful experience the men under their command suffer. And, for the most part, they bear their duty alone. On behalf of men who have served with them, I salute such officers as General Carl Hoffman and their courage in the face of unbelievable responsibility. I thank them for their friendship, encouragement, and the inspiration their lives have had upon mine and so many others.

Not long after the wedding, I received the sterling silver cup from the father of the bride. It reminds me of a charming couple and their wedding. I also remember General Carl W. Hoffman and men like him.

VI
Treasures Or Trash

TREASURES OR TRASH

Long lines of people waiting ... waiting to get shots, to be fed, to get paid, or for mail call. Sometimes even going into battle demanded a waiting line. Discovering what our men were thinking while standing in those lines became an interesting pasttime for me. There were the standard waiting games such as playing cards, swapping yarns, writing letters or grabbing forty winks.

I noticed when the air was thick with fear and danger that much of the levity was subdued and that serious evaluation of life occupied the thoughts of the men with whom I was associated. And this was certainly true of me. During one such serious waiting time I recalled a sign I had seen just outside the Marine Corps Base in Twenty-nine Palms, California. It advertised a "swapshop" of sorts. I never drove the distance to see what actually went on there, but the sign itself became the subject of or an illustration in several sermons. It read "Treasures or Trash: We Deal in Either." The implication was clear that junk to one person might be treasure to another and vice versa, and that someone was out to make money on that premise.

During waiting times that preceded potentially dangerous situations, the men juggled priorities. What had once seemed so important became of no value and that which had been taken for granted loomed invaluable. The great moments of questioning one's spiritual beliefs is not an uncommon occurrence in such waiting times. I am not sure that the tendency to turn one's thoughts to God in wartime is less than a blessing. We too easily forget God when the soul is at peace. Many of the foxhole converts are more serious about their faith after such an experience than are those who have simply grown into a religious faith. I learned, too, that even though I was a minister my thoughts were not that much different from everyone else's. It may have been simpler for me to identify all the issues with theological tags, but a Marine next to me and the commanding officer on the hill basically had the same inner struggles.

The assurance of a relationship to God seemed to be the bottom line for most men, and even that assurance seemed flimsy in light of real bullets and booby traps. For me, mouthing beliefs from the pulpit made it easy to talk to others about faith and God, but in the times of waiting, I often found the test of how strongly I believed, at hand.

It was during these times of testing that some treasures became trash and some trash, treasures. Family and self-preservation, always prized, increased in value. Material possessions and hypocrisy in the guise of wanting to "look good" became trash. Specifics of what these men were thinking depended on their background and experience. All I really knew were the questions plaguing my own heart and mind and the answers I clung to.

WHO SHALL I SAY SENT ME?

One evening after an extremely tiring day of moving into a suspected Viet Cong stronghold, two companies of our battalion were making preparations for the night. Those preparations included securing a perimeter from infiltration and providing a foxhole or some available cover for everyone before sunset. Just before the sun went down, I stopped for a few moments and leaned against the facade of an old bombed-out building. The front wall was all that remained. The sun behind my back slowly allowed the shadow of the wall to spread out in front of me. I watched the shadow grow and in those moments I recalled sitting in a church back in California where the congregation was singing "Beneath the Cross of Jesus." As the shadow crept even deeper, it slowly dawned on me that it was being cast by a cross and that the building I was leaning against had once been a church. I reached for my Bible hoping to read a few verses before daylight was gone. I knew that if the night turned into the nightmare we all expected, I would need something to say to the men. Questions leaped through my mind such as "Lord, what am I doing in this place? I can do a pretty good job back in San Diego or Waco, or just about anywhere else? ... How can the uncertainty I'm feeling allow me to be a spokesman for any kind of eternal truth?"

Ironically, I opened my Bible to the Old Testament passage where we are told of God's calling Moses to lead the children of Israel out of bondage. Moses, too, wondered how he could be a spokesman to so many. And, like Moses, I wondered, were they to ask, "What shall I say to these men about who would have me lay these words on them?" Who was

I to presume to say 'Here's the good news for today, guys.' Perhaps I needed some tracts entitled "How to Be Happy and Keep Your Wits About You in War" to distribute. I knew these men would expect more than a collection of religious cliches, more than platitudes about "pie in the sky."

What I was saying to God about being back in the States was no different from what all the men were saying. I had heard it many times before. They were scared and so was I. But I was not in Texas or California. I was in South Vietnam, and the question pounded in my brain, "What will give credibility to my efforts to encourage and sustain these men?"

I glanced down at my Bible and my eyes fell upon the plea of Moses for God to tell him who had sent him as the spokesman. It was the answer Moses received that became my answer as well ... "Tell them, I AM THAT I AM has sent you." I had read all around that scripture, never understanding it, and now, standing below a bombed-out church in the middle of a war, its meaning, its sense exploded in my head.

The Jews had names for God, most of which identified Him with a time of deliverance. Those names remained special. But here God seems to be saying, "I am still all those things you know me to be, but I am more. I am anything you need me to be in any situation." That was it! There are some things God alone can do, including answering eternal questions. In this situation, as in most, my efforts were of value only as He was allowed to work through me. All I had to do was be available. That brought me peace. From that point on, I just tried to be with the men, to let them see me as someone with the same struggles they had, caring about their needs.

I had rediscovered a valued treasure I had always

possessed - a God with all the power and the answers who stood by me, a God whom I could share with others.

WHO CARES IF YOU CARE?

I'll never forget the lesson I learned beneath the cross that evening. Whether in a church staff position, the military, everyday relationships, or at home, caring is the secret of meeting the needs around you. Practicing that caring can be fun.

The first ship to which I was assigned after leaving Vietnam was a deep-draft vessel. There were six decks down to the fire and engine rooms. The men working down there had few visitors. The ladders down to their working spaces were straight down, never the easiest route to take. The boilers of those ships, with use, became coated inside with the residue of burned fuel, and were regularly scrubbed clean. Someone had to get inside those boilers and scrape down the sides. This was usually left to the boiler tenders known as "snipes." Working inside those dark boilers around the clock, always dirty, might understandably make them feel that nobody cared about them.

One of my favorite outings was a trip taken about three in the morning, dressed in a fresh white uniform. I would descend those steep ladders, squeeze through the narrow hatch into the boiler where the men were busy, and throw my sanitized white arm around their gritty, sooty shoulders. The expressions on their faces were incredulous and they would always ask, "Chaplain, what are you doing down here at this hour — and wearing whites?" It delighted me to answer, "We just wanted you to know we care that you are down here; you have not been forgotten!" The difference in their attitudes was remarkable, and their dedication to a thankless job would become obvious, just because they knew someone cared. On one of those early morning trips down the ladders a non-commissioned officer was just ahead of me taking coffee to the men working below. I carefully followed him but about halfway down I slipped, my foot hitting the coffee pot in his hand. We had exchanged a few friendly words, but when the coffee spilled on his knee, being a bosun's mate, he had a few choice words to add. He closed his response with "Oh, for Christ's sake!" Only a moment before I had slipped he had asked me why I was going below at that time of the night. I now responded to the question ... "That's the reason. For His sake!"

Each act of caring, no matter how small, reaps a tremendous return. Someone very wise once said about achieving happiness, "If your cup runneth over, slosh a little on somebody."

VII
Wounds Robed In Splendor

WOUNDS ROBED IN SPLENDOR

Endless acres of rice paddies blanket the flat lands of South Vietnam's rice belt. In those parts of the country that are sparsely populated, wild berries, peppers, and bananas flourish along with some wild game. To me, the most enjoyable of these edibles were the bananas. Smaller than the South American variety to which Americans are accustomed, these little bananas are ready to eat while their skin is still green.

Early in 1966, three companies of Marines had moved into one of these sparsely populated areas north of the old provincial capitol of Hue. Their objective was to test the strength of opposing forces and to attempt to ascertain their numbers. "Jolly Green Giant" helicopters had brought them to the site chosen for their base of operations. The terrain was drastically different from what the Marines had been accustomed to in Chu Lai. The three to five mile visibility was a welcome change to the closed-in feeling of their home base. Since arrival was fairly early in the morning, a safe perimeter had been established before mid-morning and the men were settling in at their assigned duties. After finding a spot to dig my foxhole, I walked about trying to see as many of the men as possible.

A clump of banana trees about one hundred yards away caught my eye and, given this opportunity to supplement "C" rations, I sauntered over that way.

As I drew nearer the trees, I noticed two Vietnamese squatting in their fashion, facing one another and they appeared to be holding hands. As I got closer to the trees it became obvious that one of these men was an interrogator and the other was a prisoner. The right hand of the prisoner was lashed by a leather thong to his right ankle while the interrogator held the little finger of his left hand, bending it back over the top of his hand. When answers to his questions did not please him, the questioner would apply more pressure to the little finger of the prisoner. Finally, I had gotten close enough to hear their voices and suddenly there was a loud snap. A whimper of pain accompanied the snapping sound, and the interrogator looked up at me and smiled. The finger, now broken, dangled limply over the back of the prisoner's hand. I forgot about the bananas, and returned to finish my foxhole with the sound of the cry of pain and the snap of the finger sticking in my mind like a nail in a pine board.

The incident I had just witnessed led to disturbing thoughts of other practices, common in this land, yet so different from anything I had ever seen in the States. I am not so naive as to think that violence and inhumane treatment are never experienced in America, but I do know that they are not an accepted way of life, and that the laws of our land find such treatment in contempt of all our country stands for. Human life was not valued in Vietnam as it was back home. I thought about some of the religious practices prevalent in Southeast Asia and other parts of the world that foster the doctrine of reincarnation. That doctrine holds that a person's spirit assumes another life form, such as a dog, cat, or other creature, after death. Those who adhere to this belief fear that unless they are buried in their native soil they will become a wandering spirit. Many of the displaced Vietnamese citizens and soldiers often carried little bags of soil from their homes to be buried in should they die before they could return to their homes. Others were promised that upon their death they would be buried in shallow graves, to be retrieved later for transfer to their homes for burial. These people feared being maimed or disfigured since they believed that whatever disfigurement was inflicted on them in this life would appear in the next life form. It was not uncommon to discover bodies in those temporary graves, maimed or mutilated. This kind of treatment served as a reminder of the cruelty of this war.

The finger breaking incident and the thoughts it had prompted of other cruel acts led me to realize how grateful I am for the teachings of my faith and the general principles of humane treatment upheld by the laws of our land. I believe constant exposure to the tragic wounds of fellow Americans, plus the high incidence of vicious acts as described here, could well be a major contributing factor to the psychiatric difficulties encountered by some of our veterans. Our soldiers come from a society whose foundational tenets differ from what they have to witness elsewhere. Fortunately, though, our basic beliefs open the way for not only physical recovery, but for spiritual recovery as well. For those who have lost one or more limbs, the belief that life exists beyond this one presents an even more substantial hope, that of being made whole again. How emphatically many of our men speak—either loudly or by silent performance—of how complete is their recovery, and how important faith is in that process. Let me share with you the stories of several of these veterans.

SAM

Dr. Steve Lemons, the director of a regional Veterans Administration facility, was giving me a tour of his facility one day, when he was momentarily distracted by a business matter. I looked around for someone to visit with and noticed a young man seated behind a desk. I was almost to the desk before I realized that he was in a wheelchair. Both of his legs were missing. A brief introduction revealed a natural self-confidence and assurance that was hard to ignore. I wanted to know more about this man and his story.

Sam had gone to Vietnam as a lance corporal in 1966. He was assigned to First Battalion, First Regiment, First Marine Division, as a radio operator. Company "B" was his home away from home. Carrying the forty to sixty pounds of communications equipment demanded a physically strong individual. Sam certainly filled the bill in that regard. Sam's huge frame topped with coal-black hair made him an object of friendly curiosity among the Vietnamese children. They are small by our standards, and next to Sam they looked pitifully small. In the early years of American involvement in South Vietnam, the Vietnamese questioned the open friendliness of our servicemen. Their culture, along with certain religious beliefs, implied that doing something for someone merely meant that you wanted something in return. Suspicion was high in those days as the people asked "What are these Americans doing so far from their homeland, and what do they want?" American troops gladly shared their food rations, candy, gum and cigarettes and asked nothing in return. The Vietnamese found this kindness difficult to understand. But by the time Sam and his contemporaries arrived, being ignored by the children while walking through their village was an occurrence long since past. Each patrol or squad was met by more and more children as they passed through the little villages. The children ran along at the heels of Americans with pleading looks and impish grins ... natural heart-grabbers to most of our men. Sam became particularly popular with many of the children who never seemed to tire of watching his big frame and interesting radio equipment.

For seven months, Sam endured patrols, firefights, monsoons, and all the other unreal exigencies of war. In February of 1967 all that was to change for Sam. A battalion-sized operation into a suspected heavy concentration of Viet Cong was ordered. Early in the morning, the battalion moved out from their base south of Danang. By daylight, most of the battalion was ready to move into an area known to be laced with land mines and booby traps. Sam's company was assigned as a blocking force. They were positioned on the opposite side of the action and would attempt to block the escape of any Viet Cong who were fleeing from the forward movement of the main body.

The Viet Cong knew that the Americans were not likely to take a difficult path through the paddies but would, in all probability, take the easy path over dry land when possible. They were right, and those were the areas most heavily mined. Company "B" established its command post in a cemetery and the push began. Land mines exploded within the company area and casualties came quickly. Sam was standing near his company's commanding officer calling in casualty reports and requesting medical evacuation for the wounded. Suddenly, someone took a wrong step. A land mine exploded just behind Sam. The blast took off both legs of the company commander. Sam's right leg was severed and lay off to one side. His left leg was badly mangled. His radio equipment may have protected his upper body. Sam did not lose consciousness and, with both arms bleeding from less serious wounds, he instinctively reached out and pulled the severed right leg back into its place. He thought about death, then about his family. Then he prayed to live. He did not want to die there. Family, faith and a whole lot of stubbornness made him determined to live. Sam resolved "to go home."

More fortunate than some, Sam did come home. He came home . . . with no whimpering, no self-pity, and no regrets. Sam would go again if called. His love for his family and his country are not diminished by the loss of his legs, but, on the contrary, are enriched by the price he paid to guarantee their home and their safety.

Men like Sam do not think of themselves as heroes, even though their actions bespeak the courage and patience of quiet heroes. The great majority of them have risen above their wounds. They have moved forward facing each day's duties, doing what had to be done. Many have experienced dark dreams, been lost in their haze, only to be propelled into the light by new discoveries of strengths they did not know they possessed. For many, their faith, their belief in an afterlife promising total wholeness has carried them not only through but on to victory.

Memories of cannon and mortars echo in my heart and land mines and grenades shake the ground beneath my feet when I look upon these men. But I also see the broad stripes and bright stars of Old Glory upon them. The decades that have seen her stars increase have also felt a breeze that lifted her colors to float full and free. That breeze has been the life breath of sacrifice made by the "good soldiers" described on these pages. The marks of Vietnam's undeclared war on the bodies of these special men are, more often than not, robed in the splendor of the American spirit.

JANE

Jane's husband was a navigator, a career military officer with fourteen years of service. They lived in Bangor, Maine, where his military career had most recently taken them. Two young sons kept them busy. The Vietnam build-up had intensified and everyone lived with the apprehension of receiving orders for South Vietnam. Jane, like other military wives, braced herself for that eventuality.

Those orders arrived. One Monday morning a phone call came for her husband and, although her questions were met with evasiveness, Jane intuitively knew it concerned orders to Vietnam. Confirmation came later in the day and, with the kind of commitment typical of most military wives, the situation was accepted and preparations for resettling were begun.

Jane and the boys would go to Texas where she had family. Her husband was ordered to report to Florida on Sunday, only six days later, for six weeks of training before leaving for South Vietnam. Upon arriving, he located and rented an apartment in Florida so Jane and the boys could join him. Jane enlisted the help of a neighbor in attaching the car-top carrier to the station wagon and proceeded to pack the car with essentials for six weeks in an apartment. Because there was no time to move his family before departing for Florida, they would have to return to Bangor and move out of quarters before going on to Texas. Furthermore, they had to lease a place in Texas for the family to move into six weeks hence. All this required the renting of three places at once: Texas, Florida, and base quarters in Bangor. Despite these inconveniences, nothing was allowed to impose upon the few weeks still left to the family.

Those weeks in Florida passed all too quickly. It was not all vacation time; their special moments were squeezed in after the daily training sessions. This Vietnam-bound man needed time to share himself with wife, sons, and his mother and father who had joined them. During those days both Jane and her husband seemed to experience feelings of foreboding, feelings that he might not return. It was not an obsession, just a strong unspoken understanding between them.

All too soon he was in Vietnam, a navigator assigned to an Air Commando squadron operating out of Nha Trang. His plane was a C-47 which had been converted to a gunship for use in several types of missions. Sometimes machine gunners sat in the side doors and provided support for ground troops; at other times phosphorus flares were dropped to light up areas vulnerable to night attack. The days moved along and soon Christmas was near. Back home, Jane kept busy being mother and father to two growing boys. Accepting an unpleasant and uneasy separation is a way of life for the wives of military men. For their tenth wedding anniversary her husband enlisted his mother-in-law's assistance in presenting his Texas born wife with traditional yellow roses. Christmas was difficult with the absence of the father emphasized by his presence in war-zone Vietnam. The fears attendant to his duty were somewhat allayed by news that he was about to be assigned a desk job relieving him of his more hazardous duties. The difficulties which did exist were magnified by seemingly uncaring attitudes of friends. Some responded to the mention of a lonely Christmas without a family member, one who was in dangerous circumstances, with "Yes, we know how you feel, we have a son in Shreveport." Jane, disappointed in that kind of "encouragement," tried to pass it off as a lack of understanding.

The relief she was feeling over her husband's new assignment was shortlived. The crew he was leaving had not yet received his replacement so he volunteered to continue flying missions with them while also performing his new duties. One morning in early spring, Jane picked up the newspaper to headlines that reported "C-47 CRASHES RETURNING TO NHA TRANG: NO SURVIVORS." No names were listed, but somehow she knew. She went on to school where she was teaching. When only a short time later the principal asked her to come to his office, she was met by a military chaplain and another officer with the news. Her husband was on board that plane.

Years later, Jane still must deal with problems related to her loss and her children's loss. Refugee children have chased and spit at one son, for whatever reason. Acquaintances have remarked of her husband's death "that was his job." But in spite of the thoughtlessness added to the burden of her loss, Jane moves forward as an outstanding Christian woman with a heart open to those who need her. It is entirely in order for me to suggest that her wounds are robed in the splendor of the American spirit no less convincingly than are those of the soldiers who gave full measure. Women like Jane, heroines of a special kind, are due honor and respect.

MICHAEL

In 1969 Michael was twenty-one years old and a Green Beret sergeant in Vietnam. Green Berets were perhaps the most skilled and highly trained fighters of any war in history. Each one had a specialty and Michael's was demolition.

Michael stood about five feet eight or nine inches tall and weighed about one hundred seventy-five pounds with reddish brown hair and piercing eyes. A whole book could be written about this man, but, for our purposes, I lift just one experience out of his life. His experiences and thoughts can be multiplied thousands of times in the memories of other veterans.

It was January 3, 1969. Michael was ordered to level a hilltop with explosives and then smooth it out with a bulldozer. The pad was to be a helicopter landing area.

Shortly before this assignment, Billy, a nineteen year-old soldier was assigned to Michael's unit. Billy and Michael became good friends and by the time the helicopter pad was ordered the friendship was stronger than ever. The older Michael felt responsibility for the nineteen-year-old Billy even though there was not that much difference in their ages. But from the standpoint of experience, Michael was mature beyond his years. Billy pleaded with Michael to let him accompany him to the top of the hill. They rode off on a bulldozer, Michael operating it and Billy manning a machine gun mounted on the rear. Suddenly a terrific blast interrupted their short journey to the hilltop. They had run over a land mine, unleashing all its fury. Michael spun around quickly enough to see Billy's body blown in half by

75

the explosion. Michael suffered shattered legs and head wounds. Rescuers arrived within moments and found Michael trying to stop the bleeding from the upper portion of Billy's body.

Seventeen years later, Michael still blames himself for Billy's death. The guilt is not justified, but it reflects a sensitivity in the character of many veterans, perhaps a feeling of intense responsibility for others, born from the clutch of combat.

In 1984 Michael declined to carry the American flag in the Veteran's Day parade. His own response to those who had asked him to do so was "I am not worthy." Some of his close friends knew better. This man who thought himself unworthy to carry the flag of this country owns a Silver Star, two Bronze Stars, three Purple Hearts, a Congressional Citation, a Presidential Citation, the highest award ever given by the Republic of Korea, and the Australian equivalent of the Medal of Honor. The man is a bonafide National Hero.

He was finally persuaded to carry the flag. As they marched the parade route, an old man, at least in his eighties, was standing on the curb. When Michael approached with the flag, that dear old gentleman stood shakily at attention and, with an unsteady hand, gave a beautiful salute. Michael wept and felt good.

VIII
What Is Full Measure?

I was inwardly assured that
somewhere inside all men there is
some reservoir of strength that, when
tapped, can help them rise above
whatever storms they have to face.

WHAT IS FULL MEASURE

Following my tour of duty in Vietnam I was assigned to the Philadelphia Naval Hospital. I was surprised to get such an assignment. Having suffered a substantial weight loss and other health problems, my reactions at that time were mixed as to the wisdom of my being sent to work with Vietnam amputees and veterans with other problems. I felt I did not need to be where such great emotional stress would be a factor for me to deal with on a daily basis. I had a lot of turmoil within myself without having to minister to those who needed someone stronger. But like most fears, this one was unfounded and my assignment turned out to be the best thing that ever happened to me. Witnessing the rehabilitation processes of amputees and others with assorted wounds taught me a great deal and helped me to sort out a number of inner turmoils.

The hospital was a large facility designed to treat numerous and various injuries and illnesses. There was a series of wards which I called the "wards of invisible wounds." Those wards were set aside to house men being treated for wounds of the mind and spirit. These wounds were just as real as a physical injury, and sometimes much more difficult to treat. A missing arm or leg, a head wound, any of these can be identified and the healing and restoration processes begun. But a wound of the mind and spirit is difficult to identify, to pinpoint, to prescribe a specific treatment for. Too, when the person with these invisible wounds refuses to talk about them, the situation becomes even more complicated. Doctors and technicians often feel helpless when faced with a patient who needs help but who cannot and will not help himself. I learned lasting lessons in humanity from the wards I visited during those months watching men struggle with both wounds of the mind and spirit as well as with the loss of limbs.

An amazing thing happened to me one day, the result of such a simple impulse, yet one that revealed so much. I was on my way to the psychiatric ward to make a routine visit. The men on that particular ward were at varying stages of their recovery. Some could talk freely while others spoke to no one. In order to reach the ward, I had to pass the tennis courts where on this particular day two doctors were hard at some very serious tennis. Neither of them was very good, I noticed. As I neared the gate which led onto the courts, the player at the opposite end hit a pretty good forehand which his opponent failed to return. It made the man so angry that he threw his racquet to the ground, jumped up and down on it a few times, and then tossed it into the air. He readied to kick the racquet before it could hit the ground, but failed and instead landed on a well-cushioned part of his anatomy. Embarrassed, he got up, brushed himself off, picked up the mangled racquet, and marched resolutely out the gate where he tossed the poor instrument into the trash can. Something prompted me to rescue the racquet and I proceeded to the ward with it draped over my shoulders. When I walked into the ward with that pitiful racquet I was greeted with a barrage of questions, some from the mouths of young men who had not spoken for months to either doctors or ministers or anyone else.

It may have been the beginning of a recovery process for some of them. Even speaking of such a simple matter as a mangled tennis racquet could open the door to facing the deeply rooted struggles within. That racquet is an important item in my collection of memorabilia.

These invisible wounds are just as real as any physical wound, particularly if they are the result of combat experiences. In those instances, memories seem unreal in the silent confines of the mind, and recalling the most horrible events, those repulsive to the patient, is most difficult and painful. Our veterans hospitals are filled with men and women who are veterans of World War II, and the beds they occupy have been home to some of the vets from Korea and World War I. In many instances, these men never recovered from their invisible wounds. These men gave the full measure in service to their country. After leaving the ward with my prized tennis racquet, I headed on to the officers' ward. A young Marine lieutenant had a room on the top floor. He had been an outstanding triple-threat athlete in his home state of Pennsylvania. Now, he was a triple amputee. Both legs almost to the hip, one arm, and all the fingers on the right hand except for the index finger and thumb were missing.

My thoughts, as I had walked to the officers' ward, were of the other young men and the prayers I had for their recovery. When I entered this young officer's room, I was quickly reminded by what I saw there of the great spirit these men have exhibited in seemingly hopeless situations. I was inwardly assured that somewhere inside all men there is some reservoir of strength that, when tapped, can help them rise above whatever storms they have to face.

The lieutenant was propped up, a typewriter

where his legs should have been. Gone were those sturdy legs that had carried him swiftly through opposing tacklers on the football field. An arm that had swiftly pushed away opponents was no more. All that remained of an athlete's tools were two fingers of the hand that had thrown rifle like touchdown passes. Yet on that afternoon, with his index finger, he was typing an essay for the Freedom Foundation National Contest. I never learned how he placed in the judging of those essays, but I remember one line he let me read: "I would gladly go again, even now, and lay down the full measure of my life . . ."

The ministry at the naval hospital which I had first dreaded had transformed itself into a divine appointment, where in ministering I was ministered unto. I had seen deep wounds of the spirit and broken and torn bodies of young Americans, and I am honored and humbled by the opportunity I had just to be in their company. I had given so little, they . . . so much.

IX
The Black Irishman's Happy Hour Lives Again!

THE BLACK IRISHMAN'S HAPPY HOUR
LIVES AGAIN

One of the difficult things for me to handle, though I recognize that we all have certain rights, was the anti-war demonstrations held during the Vietnam conflict, particularly those led by some prominent personality. I never questioned their right to protest or demonstrate. But when someone like Dr. Benjamin Spock made public pronouncements that added confusion and increased burdens on those already suffering, I was offended.

While stationed at the Philadelphia Naval Hospital I ministered and was ministered to by several amputees, all freshly arrived from Vietnam. During this time, Dr. Spock conducted one of his "panty raids" on the Pentagon. He made statements which inferred that the real heroes of Vietnam were those young men who had hidden in churches and the ministers who had protected them. I strongly disagreed with him then, and still do.

Marines with less than whole bodies agreed with me, too. In fact, those Marines orchestrated a response to Dr. Spock much more eloquent than any spoken word. Nine Marines and I paid a visit to Dr. Spock. When asked to discuss his recent statements, he had nothing to say.

The incident inspired these Marines to do something to show their support for comrades still in Vietnam. They prepared four hundred boxes they called "Happy Hour" boxes, each containing anchovies, sardines, cheeses, Tabasco sauce and assorted canned goods, to be sent to Vietnam. Four men (a fire team) would share each box. Support and goods came from everywhere, but those young men raised most of the money for the project. The project, begun as a response to Dr. Spock and inspired by the stories I had told them about the Black Irishman, grew into a widespread statement to their buddies still in Vietnam . . ."you are not forgotten, we care, we support you, we understand."

The Black Irishman would have gotten a chuckle out of that project. He would also have been honored. His Happy Hour lived again.

X
Open Letter To Veterans

I believe that our nation, torn by its
most shattering experience, will after a time
of reflection and self-examination recognize
and deliver the honor and respect
Vietnam veterans deserve.

OPEN LETTER TO VETERANS
WHERE ARE THE HEROES?

One of the great tragedies of recent American history has been, in my opinion, the absence of real heroes - those honored individuals who once captured the hearts and admiration of every citizen. Their deeds, always worthy of emulation, attracted a following and established a place in history. But in the present era, non-heroes and rebels without causes tickle the fancy of our youth. For whatever reason, rebellion just for the sake of rebellion seems inordinately popular. This rebellion has spilled over into every art form, especially into the music and entertainment industry. It is as if those forms have become escapes from reality rather than methods of creativity. Many feel that hard rock music reflects Satanism and explicit, often perverse, sex. Performers who openly advocate drug use and who practice life styles less than exemplary, receive undeserved adoration from millions of our young people. In a land where freedom of expression is taken for granted, the cost of that freedom is rarely examined. Heroes who gained that freedom for our citizens seldom enjoy the widespread recognition or financial rewards that rock performers or other "stars" attain. While we stand in disbelief and disappointment at the "rebels" our children worship, perhaps this shift in idol-worship from hero to rebel may well be laid at our own feet.

Thoughts about undeserving heroes or a lack of heroes evoke memories from South Vietnam. All veterans undoubtedly remember scenes of saddened children in pitiful little villages, children with little hope and few heroes to emulate. One scene in particular has never left my mind, not even for a day, in more than twenty years. I was riding in a jeep with a driver who must have received his driver's training at a demolition derby. We were winding through a sparsely populated area that abounded with palm and banana trees. Since damage to one of those trees usually caused quite a stir and cost a substantial outlay of cash in payment for the damage, he slowed down to avoid them. As we slowed, what seemed like dozens of little children appeared from nowhere and began running along behind the jeep. Their hands were outstretched and their faces were strained and anxious. I took a short movie of those hands and faces and have viewed it many times since. The impact of that moment has never faded. With that recollection, a thousand other scenes unfold.

All little peasant villages of South Vietnam looked about the same in 1965. Schools were usually situated at some mid-point between groups of resident farmers. The schools were all closed. Children, women, and old men were usually the only persons seen in the villages. The old men were usually idle while the women were almost always busy at some form of manual labor, often carrying a bamboo pole with five-gallon cans of water balanced on either end. Every step taken caused the pole to bend and snap back so that the bearer had to effect a special rhythm to avoid spilling the water.

In all the hundreds of scenes like this, the younger men were conspicuous by their absence. They were either South Vietnam regulars, militia, Viet Cong or dead. One or two would occasionally come back to the village, work a few days for the family, and then be gone again. In some cases, this pattern would strangely and abruptly assume a different look. Overnight, a few young men would appear in a village. This would seem natural enough since they did not look any different from others who had been in and out with their families. But this time there would be an obvious tension to the change. The villagers were no longer as friendly as they had been the day before. They seemed anxious. It was almost as though they had posted a sign reading "Don't stop. Just move on through."

Our corpsmen who made daily visits to the villages to treat a wide assortment of cuts, bruises or ills would notice a bullet wound among those who stood in line for first aid. Inevitably, the one with the bullet wound would be one of those strange young men who had suddenly appeared. No questions were asked about the wound. We suspected that it probably occurred during an exchange of small arms fire with our security watch.

The South Vietnamese had over the years learned to do what was necessary to survive. They had seen benefactors, like us, come and go without effecting much change in their chances for freedom. Whenever possible, the Viet Cong would move into these little villages and terrorize and threaten the villagers into providing food and shelter for them. Threats of maiming were usually sufficient to subdue most villagers. There were instances where whole families were impaled on bamboo stakes at the entrance to a village to warn others of the folly of disobeying. Threats against the children usually kept fearful parents subservient and docile. Children were even used a shields while Viet Cong posing as villagers escaped.

On one occasion, we learned that a thatched roof house was being used as a launching pad for mortars. The attacks made from that location were in total disregard for the safety of other surrounding villages and their inhabitants. The entire area was determined unsafe until that threat could be removed. A twenty-four hour warning was issued whenever a particular village was to be destroyed so that all who lived there could seek safety. Pamphlets were air-dropped into the village promising relocation and refuge for any who desired it.

Our troops encountered machine gun fire coming from one of the grass houses as they entered the village. Return fire set the house aflame. As the little structure burned, twelve-inch thick concrete walls within the bamboo and grass outer structure were revealed. Inside, three children between the ages of eleven and sixteen had been chained to machine guns and told that Americans were coming to kill them. The men who had held the village hostage had fled long before our troops arrived. One of those three children in the house was badly burned. A Marine in that action quickly lifted the child in his arms and ran quite some distance to obtain medical attention for the child. Even though he probably saved that child's life, no one ever got his name. When the first South Vietnamese elections were held, many villagers were told that if they voted, they would never see their children again. Election day came and parents whose children had already been kidnapped stood in line to vote. One set of parents whose child had been kidnapped dared to vote despite death threats. While they were waiting in line, their child came wandering out of the woods, both hands missing.

They voted, nevertheless.

Impressions from observing these events have lingered and grown in their importance with clear lessons to be derived from them. Outstretched hands and fearful glances of the children seen in Vietnam may be manifested in other ways by their counterparts in America, but the wants and needs of all children are the same. The only difference lies in the fact that in this country, there is hope.

The tragedy of a child growing up in a land where the men are absent due to political turmoil and civil war is devastating. America's military personnel witnessed scenes in Southeast Asia that saddened their hearts and perhaps even broke the spirits of anyone who cared for the little children. But even in our society, with hope, with all the material trappings abundant, is it not just as tragic for children to be without their fathers for no other reason than that the father has simply chosen to follow another path?

If no other good comes from having been in that conflict, may it at least inspire us to care as much for the children of our land as we did for those of Southeast Asia. There are different ways of caring for and reaching out to young people. One way is to be a person with pride in appearance and with self-esteem. If I could change the drift in the type of role models, heroes, our children adopt, then I would have to begin with myself. No veteran should feel that because they were in "Nam" they have anything to hide or any reason to feel less than proud of their service. The right kind of hero gives our children a role model that lifts their spirits and whose best example is in meeting life's difficulties with head held high. You have been through hell and have returned, perhaps not in one physical piece, and certainly not as the same person who existed before "Nam," but you are alive. There is nothing you must now face any worse that what you have already faced and perhaps conquered.

I hurt with those who are openly bitter because they feel Vietnam veterans have not received adequate recognition. They obviously have suffered in unique ways that can only be explained as their having been a victim of feeling more than enough of war's heavy blows to the heart. However, until the day when the recognition and respect we are due comes, we must all conduct ourselves with the class and dignity deserving of that recognition. Our children need that of us. We must stand tall in spirit and feel good about ourselves and the service we gave our country.

I believe that our nation, torn by its most shattering experience, will after a time of reflection and self-examination recognize and deliver the honor and respect Vietnam veterans deserve. But while the nation heals, hundreds of veterans continue their lives quietly, all carrying painful memories, some carrying raging conflicts within. Most have reconciled themselves with the "real world" and with "things the way they are" and have built for themselves successful, fulfilled lives. And, we are home.

Despite the anger over lack of recognition, despite the lasting wounds, injuries to the spirit and special hurts only a Vietnam veteran and his family can know, we are home. It is what you dreamed about, longed for and thought you might never see again. You are with friends, with people willing to help, and, even though separated by distance, we are with each other, with that unique bond of kinship that is unbreakable and is forever.

And laid at our feet is the opportunity to be role models - the right kind - for our young people. Being a hero in the eyes of a nation is not as important as being the kind of hero whose life inspires another to become the best person possible.

Recently, a young man in his late twenties said to me, "I really don't know much about Vietnam." That is so true of too many other young men and women. There is a crying need for them to be told of those years that speak the truth about the madness we call war. That truth is etched in broken bodies, mangled spirits, special spots in cemeteries, empty chairs and hospital beds. But it is also written in heroic deeds of gentle men who were "good soldiers" in the most difficult of circumstances. Perhaps your work in organizations for young people, your presence in homes and businesses, your sharing of yourselves and your stories, will be the place where recognition of our deeds will begin. For wives, mothers, children, brothers and sisters who only have a memory, my prayer, as prayed by so many others, is that the passing years have tempered your hurt with some sense of purpose; for those loved ones who came home, we affirm them with love and honor which is their due.

For those who fill our veterans hospitals and need constant care, may we lift a grateful prayer equal to their measure of hurt. They were "good soldiers." These men are our heroes.

THE WAITING ROOM

Have you ever been in a waiting room while one of your loved ones was undergoing surgery? People who have understand how that period of time can seem like an eternity.

Several years ago, my wife was diagnosed as having a fibroid tumor in the uterus. Her doctor prescribed a hysterectomy in connection with the removal of the tumor. We thought that would end any concern we might have. Minor backaches and other annoying symptoms were attributed to the tumor, and its removal was something to anticipate. During our thirty-two years of marriage, this was the first major physical problem we had experienced, and we did not expect any difficulty in breezing through this development. In our minds, all would soon be back to normal.

After several hours of waiting, our physician, who was also a good friend, appeared in the waiting room and surprised us with his assessment of the situation.

"Bill," he said, "we've got a cancer."

Like everyone else who hears that word as it relates to one's own family, I was stunned. That long waiting period had been considerably shortened by the friends who sat with us, and I'll never forget them for their support. But lingering in my ears were the doctor's words, "Bill, we've got a cancer." I knew there was no way I could share the long months of chemotherapy, but I was to learn the agony of having to watch helplessly while praying for her healing and my endurance. How I would rather have had the disease myself than watch my wife suffer!

In the meantime, I saw in her a very special example of a person practicing her faith and being an enabler to those of us not so strong. More significantly, my experience in the hospital waiting room and the period of months that followed showed me the waiting time endured by military wives from a new perspective. Patiently, they have suffered through long, lonely nights, the uncertainty filling every waking moment of the necessary separation. There is an immense "waiting room" out there where women of profound strength have sustained the men of our military services with their own brand of commitment and courage.

Obviously, not all our men are what they should be, nor are all of their women. Yet in almost every instance when men are honored for their bravery and courage, strong women have been in the waiting room. It is their prayers and hopes, dreams and aspirations, that have held those men to their tasks and drawn from them their best qualities.

The partnership these women have had in the suffering of separation, in the uncertainty of relationships in the abnormalities of military life, in the fear of dreaded announcements of wounded, missing, or dead that might include the names of their loved ones — all these difficult experiences are endured by these women of our "good soldiers."

In 1964 I wrote a poem as part of an address to the National Convention of the Navy Wives Club of America in Alameda, California. I submit it here as a special tribute to the ladies of our military men, especially the wives, sweethearts, mothers, and sisters of Vietnam vets who have given these words new meaning:

TRIBUTE TO A NAVY WIFE

Sailors have worshiped in ships and in chapels,
and they've prayed on Lonely Street.
They have searched for God and found Him
where the waves of His ocean beat.
They have knelt in obscure holds
while others were busy above;
But the dearest of all their altars
were raised by a navy wife's love.
They've listened to God in the chapels,
they've caught His voice in the crowd;
They've heard Him speak when the breakers
were booming . . . crashing long and loud.
When the wind blew sharp through the mainmast,
their God spoke through the air,
But never has He spoken more clearly
than in answer to that navy wife's prayer.
The things in his life that are worthy
were born in that woman's breast,
And were breathed into his by the magic
of the love her life expressed.
The years that have brought them so close
have at times kept them apart,
But memory will keep him from straying
too far from the navy wife's heart.
God, make him the man of her vision
and purge him from selfishness.
Father, keep them true to their standards,
and help them to live to bless.
God, hallow the holy impressions
of the days that have flown as the dove.
And, Father, help him to match in kind
that navy wife's sure, incomparable love.

PASS IT ON

Our servicemen come in all shapes and sizes, colors and personality types. Ed, Bill, Joe, Charlie or Sam are all unique, and yet they all share certain common traits and characteristics. Some of our servicemen, like Joe, added their own brand of exemplary personal attributes to these traits and characteristics.

Joe grew up in the fifties and graduated from high school in 1969 as a campus leader and athlete. At sixteen he became a Christian during a Billy Graham crusade. His profession of faith grew as his commitment deepened. At Purdue University, Joe maintained a 5.82 grade point average out of a possible 6.0 in his major area of study, research chemistry. Joe was an achiever and in everything he tackled he utilized all his talents. His Christian commitment, first made publicly, was lived publicly and he was a beneficial influence wherever he went.

In 1964 Joe graduated from Purdue, married Carolyn, a self-starting achiever in her own right, and entered pilot training in the Air Force. He graduated at the head of his class at Chandler Air Force Base in Mesa, Arizona. Their first child, a son, was born in 1965.

He distinguished himself as one of the Air Force's finest instructors. Eventually, he was sent to Southeast Asia. From a base in Thailand, he flew 128 successful missions over Southeast Asia in a F105 Thunderchief. Joe spent eighteen months in Thailand. On his only thirty-day leave, he flew home to be with family and friends. During that leave, he and his family spent many hours reflecting on the pain and killing associated with war. For Joe, squaring that pain and killing with his faith was a hard struggle. Like so many others, he found concrete answers elusive. But the belief that the cause itself was just and right helped him and his family understand his duty, his missions, his purpose.

In the early 1970's American involvement in Vietnam was winding down. It was the beginning of the end of our direct involvement in this particular struggle against tryanny. Joe was transferred to Kadena Air Force Base on Okinawa. He was assigned to a special "ready" group prepared to return to Vietnam immediately if necessary. His family could now join him but were forced to live in substandard housing until base housing became available. Joe was able to fly home to visit his gravely ill father who died just several months later. His brother Ron had just experienced a painful divorce. It was a sad and unsettled time for the family.

By Christmas, though, things seemed to be improving. The family was able to move into base housing, Joe had escaped serious injury in Vietnam, and his mother was with them for Christmas. For the next several months, life passed quietly.

In March, Joe and Carolyn visited a seaside park and took a long walk along the seashore. All of the events that had taken their toll on Joe and the family during the first year resurfaced. They talked about many things, including death and loss, and the unpredictability of both. A wave uncovered an unusually large rock lodged in the sand. Joe stubbornly pulled at it until he finally wrenched it free ... it was almost as if the rock represented the roots, the permanence we all seek; possessing it seemed to give him a small sense of peace.

The next morning Joe was scheduled to fly in a two plane formation simulating a bomb attack.

When the bombs were released, the planes were to pull out and roll into a full-power climb. His plane didn't make it. A malfunction caused the plane to crash, canopy down, at 500 knots. It exploded upon hitting the water. Nothing was recovered of the plane or its occupants.

The military has a very precise and tender procedure when next of kin must be told of a death. Carolyn, busy at home with routine chores, glanced up and through the window saw two officers coming up the sidewalk. She knew their mission. She frantically closed and locked doors and windows, screaming, "Go away! Go away!" But the officers waited; they understood. When she was ready, she opened the door and the officers entered. She had to face what they had to say.

At home, Joe's brother Ron had to make the longest fifteen-mile trip he had ever driven. Followed by the colonel who had brought the news and who would make his official condolences, Ron prepared to tell his mother, a recent widow, of her son's death.

Ron and his mother wept. In Okinawa, Carolyn and her children wept. The price of having a good soldier in the family is high.

Memorial services were conducted both in Okinawa at the little church Joe and Carolyn had attended and at Joe's home church where he had grown up. Joe was dead. But the impressions he had made on people all of his life continued on. His public commitment of his life to God had touched many. At the home church memorial service a former high school classmate, influenced by the testimony of Joe's life, committed his life to God.

Joe's personal example of a life undergirded by faith, commitment, responsibility and dignity exemplified the term serviceman.

To his own son, Monte, and to Ron's son, Kendall, Joe passed on the spirit of the dedicated serviceman. Monte is currently in basic training in the Marine Corps. Kendall is a helicopter mechanic serving in various locations, presently Houduras and El Salvador. Both are committed, like Joe, to the struggle against tyranny.

Life goes on. Carolyn has remarried, Ron has remarried, sons pursue their own lives. But the pride, the commitment, the love, care and prayer Joe believed in and shared is reflected in the lives and lifestyles of the special individuls to whom he passed it on.

XI
Moving Into Reality

MOVING INTO REALITY

Fifteen to twenty years beyond the sands of Vietnam, the spirit of survival that brought many soldiers home safely, seems to have turned into a drive toward self-destruction. Overcoming what seems insurmountable wounds of the body and heart takes either a progressive positive path or one of regression and bitterness. Those who surmount their problems have faced reality ... taken their dealt hand and built on its potentials. Those who merely "cope" let circumstances dictate the hand. And still others, ongoing tragedies of the Vietnam War, live out each day dressed in combat regalia, refighting battles, recounting warfare skills. For them, the past never ends.

But the war is over and life does go on. The way each veteran deals with his or her life is a personal, free choice. The two stories that follow illustrate the choices two veterans made. Neither one had an easy road to walk. Both, however, realized successful results. Moving back into the "real world" is sometimes as painful as any battlefield experience that Vietnam, Korea or any other war can give us. Running from reality, however, may be the longest, most painful road a person can follow.

WILL THEY STOP AT MY DOOR TONIGHT?

She had loved him since she was thirteen and he was fifteen years old. Dave was a handsome youngster but no more so than Brenda was beautiful. Dave's father pastored the Lake Worth Assembly of God Church near Fort Worth, Texas, and there their early interest in one another blossomed into a truly great love story.

When Brenda was eighteen they married and Dave soon enrolled in the seminary to prepare for the ministry, his chosen career. He secured full-time work to cover school and living expenses. The job soon became very lucrative and began to sidetrack Dave from his primary objective. At the same time, the Vietnam build-up was menacing and the draft loomed over everyone, including Dave. A more permanent sidetrack saw Dave drafted and headed into the Navy. He ended up with Special Forces training with a Seal team in San Diego. The specific objective of this training was to prepare men for riverine warfare in South Vietnam. Their assignments involved patrolling the inland waterways in small boats to prevent infiltration of enemy supplies and forces. Rigorous training of these teams was perhaps as demanding as any offered in any branch of the service. As difficult as the training was, however, the most difficult task was saying goodbye to Brenda, a task for which no training was offered.

South Vietnam was half a world away and in no way resembled Dave's peaceful home. Only in retrospect could he realize the strength and resources afforded him from family support and Brenda's love across the distance. But for Dave, all sense of love, place and tomorrow seemed to end one day on a steamy little river in the heart of South Vietnam. A small river craft was quietly patrolling the river when one of the men spotted a possible enemy bunker. Phosphorus grenades would be used to burn out the weeds and provide smoke cover for the men on the boat. Dave's boat nosed into the river bank as he pulled the pin on a grenade. He was holding it near the right side of his face, preparing to throw it, when something - perhaps it was a sniper's bullet crashing through the back of his hand - detonated the grenade. Like a scene in slow motion, the resulting destruction was etched in detail forever for Dave and the men witnessing the moment.

The explosion almost took his head off. The entire right side of his face was gone. From the waist up, most of his skin was stripped away. He could actually hear his flesh sizzling like frying bacon. He looked down to where his chest had been, his right hand dangling from his wrist by a thin strip of flesh. He felt the water around him giving no coolness and he grasped at the burning flesh floating on its surface, knowing it was his. Later he would suffer blindness and deafness in his right eye and ear. He was dying and the only word on his lips was "Jesus" and then, "God, I still believe in You."

Instinctively, Dave crawled out of the water, his body still burning. By the time a rescue team appeared, he was presumed dead. He was placed on a stretcher. As the evacuation team was transporting him to the helicopter, his smoldering flesh burned through the canvas and he fell to the ground. Finally on board a helicopter and airborne, the corpsman began making out Dave's death report. In defiance, a huge groan rumbled from out of his throat, startling the pilot and crew who could not believe life still existed in the mangled body they were carrying.

Immediate medical attention served only as a first step to survival. Recovery was still a question with evacuation to the states nothing more than just possible prolongment of agony.

At a stopover in a Japanese hospital, Dave saw his reflection in a mirror for the first time and was devastated. He could not imagine his young wife still loving him and he pulled what he believed to be life support tubes from his arms. He referred to himself as "it" and could not see himself as a person. He wished he could die.

Eight days later he arrived in San Antonio with thirteen other men in similar serious circumstances. In ninety days, only one of the thirteen would still be alive. For eight months his home would be the Intensive Care Unit.

On the day following Dave's injury, Brenda and her family had attended the church in Fort Worth where she and Dave had married. Because they left early, they had missed the white-uniformed Navy Captain who delivered the news of Dave's wounds to his father. The officer then went to Brenda's home where Brenda, only twenty, realized all too soon what his message might be. But wounds, not death, were the words that stayed reality.

The first report of "minor injuries" was quickly replaced by the corrected message. The truth - thirty seven percent of his body had suffered third-degree burns, blast damage to the upper trunk, face, hands and arms was extensive, and severe cornea damage to the right eye - left his condition listed as "guarded."

Brenda went to her room to be alone and to marshal her strengths. Understandably shocked, she sought the Source of inspiration and strength and determined to be whatever Dave needed her to be.

111

She emerged from her room with a sense of peace that seemed to envelop her. Her love and devotion to Dave and her faith transformed this beautiful young woman into a rock of strength.

On the day Dave arrived in San Antonio, Brenda was waiting, anxious to hold him in her arms once more. Not knowing what to expect, she held fast to the love she had for him. She walked through the burn center at the hospital, seeing men so badly scarred that their humanity was barely discernible.

Brenda knew that Dave would be wondering if she could still love him. She tenderly plotted ways to remove all doubt from his mind. Once the door was opened for that first visit she saw him ... blackened flesh with white medication smeared all over him, face swollen, hardly recognizable. She ran to him, kissed him and said, "Welcome home, Davey." Relief flooded through Dave's mind that she had not turned away. He knew, though, what he looked like, and he offered Brenda release from their wedding vows. Brenda assuaged his doubts one by one, even as other bits of news forced more obstacles upon them. They were told his vocal chords were so damaged he might never talk again and that he would be blind in one eye and deaf in one ear. These were critical diagnoses to fling at a man who already doubted his desire to live. For Brenda, the guest wing near David's ward became "home" for weeks upon weeks. The long nights were fearful times for her. Lying in the quietness of her room, almost every night she would awaken from a restless sleep to hear the footsteps of two men walking quietly down the hall. The repetition of that experience had made her familiar with the routine. A chaplain and a doctor were going to one of the rooms to deliver news that someone had died. Their soft knock at a door was always followed in a moment by sounds of sorrow and grief. Brenda's awareness of what this routine meant was shared up and down that hall. "Will they stop at my door tonight?" was the question carried on the heartbeats of those waiting in each guest room. As the steps would pass the doors, Brenda could almost hear the sighs of relief from each one spared once again. But with relief came a sense of guilt that the ease of her personal fears came at the expense of someone else's sorrow.

Months later and thirteen major surgeries endured found Dave and Brenda faced with still another setback. They were told that they would not be able to have children. The years have tested Brenda and Dave repeatedly, but the love that binds them is established on a foundation far deeper than outward appearances. Like the love God has for us, Dave and Brenda love each other for who they are and what they are, a love of the heart rather than of the outer trimmings. Had their destinies been reversed, no one doubts that Dave would be standing by his Brenda, who, in his words, had literally opened the door for him to come back to life.

Each obstacle, each closed door, must be faced and dealt with. Dealing successfully with what waits behind our doors depends in great part on our own sense of worth. A sense of personal worth is invaluable. To be loved for our personhood is the most wonderful treasure we have. Those persons who do not have such regard for themselves need the help of others to achieve it. Those who do have that treasure must always be ready to share it. Love and caring for others more than self is the quickest road to obtaining the treasure. Reality is where we are, what we have, and where we are going. It is not where we were, what is missing, and where we have been.

Reality, perhaps, is in whether we open the door at all.

Today, Dave can see out of his eye with perfect vision. He hears from a once deaf ear. His voice, once thought lost, is an asset he uses to preach the Word of God and the knuckles of his hands beat out a mean piano tune. Two beautiful children, one with a face just like a young teenager who fell in love with a thirteen-year-old Brenda, bear witness to overcoming seemingly insurmountable odds. Dave and Brenda beat the odds, not easily, and not alone. They opened the door to face their own reality and now continue to open doors for others. Good soldiers, His good soldiers, always reach for the door first.

COMBAT COMMITMENTS RECLAIMED

James was born and raised in Fairmount, Indiana. After high school graduation, he enlisted in the Air Force and was trained to serve in the Special Forces. He also rained as an electrician.

Eventually, because of the times, he landed in Vietnam as a sergeant assigned with six other Americans as an advisor to a one hundred sixty-three man South Vietnamese paratroop unit. With patrols and other unit activites, James had little opportunity to use his skills as an electrician. On one special occasion, though, it did come in handy.

On December 22, 1965, Bob Hope's Christmas show came to Saigon, South Vietnam. James wanted very much to see it, even though seeing the show meant traveling 200 miles. James, determined he would see it, hitched a ride on a supply helicopter and then made connections on a C-47 loaded with others going to the show.

Once in Saigon, James began to figure a way to get a good seat. He volunteered to use his electrician's training to help set up the electrical equipment in return for a front row middle seat. He got that seat and a chance to sing with Anita Bryant. Everyone enjoyed the show and hated to see it end. Bob Hope's shows really brought a little bit of home to the troops and we all hated to see him leave. Just before the last musical number of the performance, James was called to immediately return to his unit. As he left his conspicuous seat, he was clinging to the words of the songs and glancing back at Bob and some of the troupe. Twelve thousand men and women attended that show and, even when he was out of sight, the strains of "Silent Night," sung by that crowd still rang in his ears.

On the way to the airfield, he learned the reason for his being called back. His camp had been attacked by a large enemy force and every one assigned was needed. Checking his weapons, the sergeant began preparing himself mentally for what might be waiting. For two and one-half hours, he waited patiently for the plane to reach Pleiku. There he transferred to a helicopter. As the chopper prepared to land at his camp, a direct hit struck the aircraft killing both the pilot and co-pilot. On impact James was thrown clear, uninjured, and made his way one hundred yards to the perimeter of the camp. He quickly assessed the situation, the expected heavy rains and enemy movements. It was not unusual for the two to be simultaneous, as air support was less likely to be available if the weather was bad enough. The Viet Cong liked to take advantage of that situation. He began immediate deployment of men and ammunition. Early on the morning of December 23, the rains came and so did the enemy. All day long incoming artillery persisted and inflicted heavy casualties. More than fifty percent of the unit were counted among the dead and wounded. Replinishing the dwindling supplies of ammunition and evacuation of the wounded and dead were impossible. The heavy Southeast Asian rains, nonexistent visibility, and the eternal chill from being wet for long periods of time, all coupled with an invisible enemy, made Christmas seem a thousand years away. During lulls in the fighting the Americans and South Vietnamese who had been taught carols sang Christmas songs. In the meantime, the Viet Cong rang bells and blew horns in an effort to frighten their enemy. Eerie as they were, these bells and horns seemed to create accompaniment to the carols.

It was a strange time-Christmas carols, bells and horns, rain and war.

The weather was the same all over the country, and radio pleas for help were fruitless. December twenty fourth was a carbon copy of the twenty-third, with losses in men and supplies mounting. It became obvious that, one way or another, it would all be over by Christmas Day. By midnight, James had distributed the last of the ammunition when he was struck in the side by a bullet. Fortunately, no internal organs were damaged, but bleeding was profuse. He crawled to his bunker and stuffed a gun rag in the open wound.

James, sitting in the mud, an empty weapon in his hand, and blood running down his side, thought of his father, mother, and two sisters, and he started crying. His soft weeping soon became heavy sobbing, wracking his body. He was inwardly shaken by the thought of never seeing his family - or another Christmas - again. He recalled what his parents had taught him to do when he needed help and he prayed. He prayed, making promises, expressing hope for survival. Then, as suddenly as it had begun, the rain stopped and so did the attack. The strains of "Silent Night" drifted faintly down the picket lines. Each man joined in and echoed what words he knew. Never had a song delivered a message so clearly.

As soon as he gained his composure, James joined in the singing. He still remembers how the sky cleared and the stars were so very bright that night. One hundred men had died in that three-day attack and all the others had been wounded at least once. The rest were alive, James believed, because the Lord had heard his prayers, and answered them.

Most veterans can recall how they, at least once,

made such commitments. Some commitments have lasted, while others, once back at home and safe from war, may not have stood the test of time.

James came back to the "real world." Readjusting didn't come easily and, among other things, he became a member of the Oakland chapter of Hell's Angels. He got married and had a little girl. When the baby was two years old, James' wife left him and the baby. James tried to be a good father, even seeing to it that his child's request to attend church was met every Sunday. As a matter of fact, on some Sundays, if his hangover was not too severe, he would even attend with her.

Years passed and his little girl's persistence paid off. The commitment made by a battle-weary soldier so long ago and lost in the shuffle of a subsequent downhill slide, finally cried out for attention in such a way that James had to respond.

Instead of hoisting a few beers with friends one Sunday evening, James answered a small, pleading little voice in the back of his mind. Perhaps it was the echo of a little girl's plea, "Daddy, please come to church with me." In an almost involuntary action, James surprised his now thirteen-year-old daughter by his invitation to go to church. That evening some young people who had been to a retreat shared fresh experiences and challenged all present to make and keep meaningful vows.

James, now safe from the blaring noises and dangers of war, reclaimed the vows first voiced near Pleiku with death just around the corner. This time, though, the commitment came with no strings attached, no restrictions on what he would or would not do "if God came through."

James stands about six feet two inches with a bald head and a beard that covers his face and, in addition, makes its appearance with a jublilant statement in style. The beard must be a foot wide at its bushiest point and is topped by a waxed handlebar moustache seven or eight inches in length. Bright blue eyes peer impishly from beneath a western hat. A marked gentleness of demeanor creates a paradox of power and tenderness. He is a craftsman. From bits and pieces of leather he fashions beautiful belts and other leather goods. His skilled fingers take broken pieces and mend them like new. From the broken fragments of a commitment made on a nightmarish Christmas Eve in 1965, James has slowly put back together his life. He stands ready to share with and to tell others of the One who created us, who can mend the brokenness and skillfully refashion a thing of beauty and purpose.

Many a veteran might do well to reclaim commitments made so long ago in another time and place. A man does not necessarily have to be at war on a battlefield to yearn for peace. In the quietness of a broken or sterile life or in the fast lane of a downhill slide, a reclaimed commitment can bring a sense of contentment and more peaceful reality than can any other path. One's wartime foxholes are things of the past - but commitments made then and renewed today can move a person into reality - a promising and hopeful tomorrow.

James and Dave and Brenda - and so many others - have opened doors, reclaimed vows, built successes on circumstances they could not change. Moving into reality may not be easy, but once you get there, it's like standing on a mountain with a clear view all around.

XII
Look Away To Distant Hills

LOOK AWAY TO DISTANT HILLS

Every person who served in Vietnam lives with memories. These memories are different, depending on the part of the country in which they served, their particular assignment while there, and the intensity of their involvement in combat. Those who served in areas near larger cities and in certain skill jobs saw little, if any, combat. Their duties were extremely important to the American effort in Vietnam, but did not evoke the kinds of feelings and emotional stress incurred by those who were in combat. Such simple amenities as indoor toilets and plumbing, usually available in cities and rare in the rural areas, made degrees of physical comfort much different. All jobs were important, but some were more physically and psychologically demanding than others. The intensity and frequency of combat experience constitute the most serious and lasting element of memories.

For some the days were serene and the nights filled with terror, while to others nighttime gave respite to weary bodies. Still others were in situations where both night and day were hellish nightmares. Some made no contact with the enemy while others saw too much of him. A few special veterans carry the memory of languishing in North Vietnamese prisons. Distinctive groups of Vietnam veterans existing today reflect the varying experiences our men encountered. There are those who seek public recognition for themselves and their comrades. To them we owe the debt of keeping alive the issue of our POW's and MIA's. Others stay silent, preferring to let the past be the past, living out their lives apart from any Vietnam ties. Still another group dwells in the agony of memories too painful to recall but too real to be put away and forgotten.

All veterans, whether Army, Air Force or Navy, share recollections that are similar, yet unique to the specific branches. Since I served with the Marines, it is from that perspective that I draw the observations shared here. For us, the nights brought the bitterest of memories and the most frightening of times. My lesson in "night fear" came one evening when two companies of our battalion deployed in a suspected enemy area. It was north of Hue and at that time no American force of any size had ever been that far north in search of the enemy.

Late in the evening we arrived at a selected site which would serve as the base for this operation. After securing the perimeter, a staff meeting was called. We gathered outside the battalion commander's tent and heard intelligence reports. We were told that we could expect a mortar attack around midnight and perhaps a testing action to detect weaknesses in our defenses. If so, the enemy would attempt to overrun the camp using machine guns, hand grenades and meat hooks. The colonel closed the meeting with the words, "Make sure everybody has an adequate foxhole."

He was talking right down my alley. I certainly wanted an "adequate foxhole." Before the briefing I had worked on my foxhole, but now I returned to recheck its adequacy. I discovered that it was not long enough for me to stretch out in, forcing me to bend my knees and lie on my back. (A foxhole is meant to protect men from mortars, and that means it must be large enough to allow the occupant to be below the surface of the ground. A mortar shell explodes on contact and scatters shrapnel parallel to the ground. If your body is below the surface, then you escape any wounds unless the shell is a direct hit.) The first order of business the next morning, I planned, would be to lengthen my inadequate foxhole. By now it was getting dark, so I rolled out a blanket beside my hole and stretched out to look at the stars, a wary eye and ear peeled for any unexpected movements or sounds. Propped up on one arm, I saw a bright light flash from behind a nearby hill. A mortar round quickly followed, belching out destruction everywhere. Everyone knew that that first round signaled many more to come. About thirty rounds pelted the camp area. With that first flash and roar I had rolled into my foxhole, knees propped up, ready to wait out the barrage. But the first missile landed square in my foxhole, and, thank God, was a dud. Suffice it to say, I evacuated that foxhole on the double. From that time on, I always had the longest, most adequate foxhole in camp. Those first shots from carbines, automatic weapons or mortars, and hand grenades planted fear of the purest sort in my brain and, from then on, even the slightest noise turned loose my instincts to seek cover. The long nights to come offered for me an uneasy sleep at best.

After the terror of the night, the hills of South Vietnam always looked so good in the morning as the sun's rays began to outline them in gold. The fog and mists rising from the little valley floors and paddy lands would become visible. But it was those first tints of light on the distant hills which were the most welcome for me. Then I could believe that out

125

beyond those hills there were people and lands untouched by this conflict.

The daylight hours would be spent getting ready for another night, but the sun felt good and warm, and promised a few safe hours. Those feelings were not just mine alone. I would watch the men as they began to stir and set about their routines. Patrols would return from long nights in the paddies or on some trail. The men looked tired and haggard and I was glad that they could get a little rest. My memories include faces of our men who died on those hills and in those valleys, too. Those of us who came home left there a part of ourselves, and my mind reaches deep to pull up images and faces of the men who shared those nights and those hills and valleys with me. I remember the young man from Philadelphia who served as my bodyguard. He had been raised in an orphanage and was one of the most genuinely good young men I have ever known. His "profanity" consisted of a word he invented which I've used many times since ... "fil-a-rac-a-pac-a loomis." By the time you got the word out, your anger had subsided.

A very young Marine lieutenant's face is as clear in my mind today as if we had been together this morning. He commanded a platoon with the responsibility of securing the airport against the infiltration of suicide squads. The last time I saw him, he was being removed from a helicopter, lying on a stretcher, with a deep wound in his upper thigh.

I see a familiar face working in a supply depot in Danang. His name was Roger Staubach.

Another familiar face gliding by in my memory is that of an Italian fellow, rugged in appearance, crew-cut, and neat as a pin, even in battle fatigues. He maintained a tough exterior, but the heart of this executive officer was warm and responsive.

I see the faces of several lieutenant colonels and battalion commanding officers, all highly intelligent men whose primary concerns were in getting the job done with the least amount of grief or human suffering. They carried these monumental responsibilities quietly and with ceaseless attention to detail.

On a forced march one day, I was close behind the radioman who was required to stay near the commanding officer. I marveled at the young man's dexterity in handling the cumbersome equipment, managing the rough trails, and never falling behind.

I see four black Marines who took it upon themselves to look after me - their smiles, their dice games, their close friendship from which they each took strength.

I see a black Marine from one state and a white Marine from another, huddled together during a mortar attack one night. They laughed at what a stir that picture would make in their respective hometowns.

There was the young bachelor dentist who learned the name of a beautiful young woman who had sent her picture to me requesting the name of a Marine with whom she could correspond. Since she was a dental technician, I thought they would have lots in common. She was a former Miss Lebanese California and we all believed she was much too beautiful to seek romance with a man she had never seen. Three years later I stumbled onto them in Japan. They had been married a year.

Another beauty contestant from Pennsylvania received a letter every day from a youngster from Arkansas in our unit. We all thought he had terminal acne and assured him he had no chance for this beauty. He had the last laugh on us; they married the next year.

Another memory leaps out of a late night patrol when I witnessed a corpsman saving a young Vietnamese woman's life. The woman had been struck in the throat by a sniper's bullet. The corpsman in that squad performed an emergency tracheotomy on her with a pen knife, saving her life.

These men, from towns all across the United States, from rich, poor or middle class families, some educated some not, red, brown, black or white, all experienced the long days and nights of Vietnam. They manned heavy weapons, used small arms, scalpels, surgical instruments, Bibles, mess gear and communications equipment. Among their number were water treatment experts, demolition technicians, supply personnel, pilots and plane crews, public relations and news persons, and medical teams. With all these differences between them, they had one common bond ... they were at war in a foreign land. Ironically, these men and women were an accumulation of expertise in all the fields necessary to run a city, and that is what most of them are doing today.

Then and there, however, they learned that the skills of war were not the only ingredients of a "good soldier." The one absolute essential was being in one's place in spite of personal fear.

At one time or another, they too glimpsed those sunkissed hills and, if all went well for them, they came home to the "real world."

It appears to me that in whatever capacity you served, at least once in that tour you must have made some kind of commitment; your faith may have been challenged, and in that moment of dark reality, a new and fresh hope crept in like the sun on those dark mountains.

Whether the days or the nights carried the most fear for you, the darkness of the experience shared by all is balanced for some of us ... we are home. That gives fresh opportunity to appreciate this country of ours. I do not have the time to demonstrate, nor do I want or need recognition. However, I have utmost respect for those who feel forgotten and a strong desire for them to receive the recognition they deserve.

I still see those distant hills bathed in the light of a new day. They are fresh in my memory. The message born in my darkest hour and nurtured as the light crept over those distant hills still refreshes me. May it inspire you to renew your faith - to meet your challenges - to fight the good fight.

LOOK AWAY TO DISTANT HILLS

To look away to distant hills while they are bathed
in light,
Brings hope to those who've walked alone in the
valleys of the night.
The shadows that snuff out the glow of a broken
heart's warm blaze,
Introduce the chance to look with hope to
brighter, better days.
The light that crowns those gleaming hills may seem
too far to acquire,
But it may be the gleam of a nearer flame that can
set your heart on fire.
Don't despair when dreams are smashed, and no
victory is in sight,
But look away to distant hills while they
are bathed in light.
Could be the light you see is one that God
Himself put there,
For you to know that cloudy days will before
long again be fair.
You have the light to guide your steps and help
you see what's right,
If you look away to distant hills while they are
bathed in light.
That look will give you compassion for those
who toil in vain;
Those who are struggling through the human race
and feeling unending pain.
So keep to the Source that first called to your
heart, and know that He still is,
And one day you will stand on those distant hills
And know that Light was His.

Know too, my friends, that you were
His "good soldiers." .... Love, Chaps

75660 9
20519
30753
B Bracelet watch